# Creating a
# Teacher Collective

# Creating a Teacher Collective

## Professional Development within the Group, the Community, and the Network

Maria Impedovo, Karen Ferreira-Meyers, and Noriyuki Inoue

ROWMAN & LITTLEFIELD
*Lanham • Boulder • New York • London*

Published by Rowman & Littlefield
An imprint of The Rowman & Littlefield Publishing Group, Inc.
4501 Forbes Boulevard, Suite 200, Lanham, Maryland 20706
www.rowman.com

86-90 Paul Street, London EC2A 4NE

Copyright © 2023 by Maria Impedovo, Karen Ferreira-Meyers, and Noriyuki Inoue

*All rights reserved.* No part of this book may be reproduced in any form or by any electronic or mechanical means, including information storage and retrieval systems, without written permission from the publisher, except by a reviewer who may quote passages in a review.

British Library Cataloguing in Publication Information Available

**Library of Congress Cataloging-in-Publication Data**

Names: Impedovo, Maria, 1984– author. | Ferreira-Meyers, Karen, author. | Inoue, Noriyuki, 1962– author.
Title: Creating a teacher collective : professional development within the group, the community, and the network / Maria Impedovo, Karen Ferreira-Meyers, and Noriyuki Inoue.
Description: Lanham, Maryland : Rowman & Littlefield, 2023. | Includes bibliographical references.
Identifiers: LCCN 2023008380 (print) | LCCN 2023008381 (ebook) | ISBN 9781475869361 (cloth) | ISBN 9781475869378 (paperback) | ISBN 9781475869385 (ebook)
Subjects: LCSH: Professional learning communities. | Teachers—Professional relationships.
Classification: LCC LB1731 .I376 2023  (print) | LCC LB1731  (ebook) | DDC 371.1—dc23/eng/20230324
LC record available at https://lccn.loc.gov/2023008380
LC ebook record available at https://lccn.loc.gov/2023008381

Without a minimum of hope, we cannot so much as start the struggle.

—P. Freire, *Pedagogy of Hope*

# Contents

Acknowledgments ix

Introduction 1

## PART I

1 Creating a Teacher Collective 7

2 Entering into a Teacher Collective 25

3 Socialization into a Teacher Collective 43

4 Development of a Teacher Community 55

5 How to Connect in a Teacher Community 69

6 Expanding a Teacher Community 81

7 Move On: The End of a Community 95

## PART II

8 Teacher Education in the Global South and Open-Source Hardware 111
  *Amit Dhakulkar and Karen Ferreira-Meyers*

9 A Boat on the River: The Case of Teacher Autonomy, Professional Development, and Online Communities 135
  *Mandana Arfa-Kaboodvand and Karen Ferreira-Meyers*

10 Community Facilitation for Social Justice Education 151
  *Aspasia Dania*

Conclusion: Passion, Action, Collaboration, and Reflection: Imperative Insights for Teacher Collectives 165
*Sally Wai-Yan Wan*

About the Authors 173

# Acknowledgments

This text was born from the fortuitous collaboration of three researchers in three different locations: France, Japan, and Eswatini. Two colleagues have never met in person, and two only once in 2017 in Cameroon, where the collaboration began and developed over time. Other colleagues from Greece, Iran, India, and Hong Kong enriched the contributions.

With this, we want to indicate how a collective is both strong and fragile. Yet, it can overcome barriers and difficulties due to internal conditions (e.g., motivations, communication) and external conditions (e.g., lack of support, funding, difficult work conditions). The group, the community, and the network are perspectives to be animated and shaped with one's participation. The collective creates and remodels itself continuously. Technology makes possible the expression of individuality and collectivity in multiple forms. The most apparent form of collective-born and collective-oriented technology is the internet.

As a reminder, in 1969, the U.S. Department of Defense decided to create a communication system that was able to exchange information between computers scattered throughout the United States and that could remain performant even in the event of a world war. The internet was born. Groups, communities, and networks were ready to go live. And so, people are ready to connect based on their mutual interests. Today, learning webs are made live through real, mediated, and hybrid connections—as theorized already by Illich in 1971:

> The operation of a peer-matching network would be simple. The user would identify himself by name and address and describe the activity for which he sought a peer. A computer would send him back the names and addresses of all those who had inserted the same description. It is amazing that such a simple utility has never been used on a broad scale for publicly valued activity. (p. x)

In the same way, all the authors of this book are connected by a topic, a passion, and an interest mediated by somewhat random personal relationships during conferences or primarily over social media channels. We developed an embryonal learning collective, oriented to challenge our comprehension of teacher professional development and learning.

## REFERENCE

Illich, I. (1971). *Deschooling society*. Harper & Row.

# Introduction

The COVID-19 pandemic has reinforced the crucial role of learning design, indicating the need to rethink lesson design to ensure innovative engagement in an increasingly globalized context (Morris & Stommel, 2018). The pandemic has also reminded us of the need to update teachers' competencies to meet 21st-century challenges (Caena & Redecker, 2019).

This book addresses the following challenge: How do we create and sustain a teacher community? For practitioners, the main question in this handbook is: How do we build and facilitate teacher communities?

The different chapters discuss teacher interaction for learning and professional development in light of three constructs: the group, the community, and the network.

A wealth of literature exists, especially on theoretical frameworks, success factors, and barriers to participation in teacher communities. However, this book addresses the need for a step-by-step guide with valuable suggestions for those who want to create (from scratch) and support a community of teachers brought together to deal with specific issues and, importantly, mediated by educational technology.

The general terms "teacher" and "teachers" used in the book must be considered from the perspective of both student-teachers and in-service teachers.

The seven chapters in part 1 of this book accompany practitioners in creating and sustaining a teacher collective: from entering a community to socialization, developing into a collective, consolidating competencies and knowledge, and finally leaving the collective.

Moreover, the book invites its readers to build and organize connections, links, and possible dialogues between concepts and metaphors to explore teacher learning and professional development in complexity. In each chapter, the current complex context of teaching is evoked by a conceptual reference, a technology, and a metaphor.

Each chapter is organized in two parts: the first links the collective to a group, community, and network; the second proposes to address the collective through a concept, technology, and metaphor for reflecting on, applying, and implementing collaboration.

In the first part of each chapter, our role is to increase active engagement in a collective. We analyze three modalities: resources, attitudes, and knowledge. These three lenses or perspectives help shape our focus on organizing activities and on the potential role of each participant. Also, knowing these three perspectives and how we want to use them give us tools to observe, model, and change learning dynamics.

In the second part of each chapter, practical concepts, technological tools, and images/metaphors are evoked to give a practical perspective on teacher professional development (TPD).

This book is intended to be read as a cartography of themes; the authors do not claim it to be exhaustive. Table I.1 gives a summary of the main concepts. Importantly, we would like to stress our position on the dynamic and changing environment of teacher professional development: we only trace some directions and propose reflections that the readers could use as the basis of their transformative aims and goals.

In table I.2, we provide some concepts that are helpful to keep in mind as perspectives suited to the theme of each chapter and that, in some way, can guide learning design.

In part 2 of the book, invited chapters give concrete examples on how to apply concepts, technologies, and prospects. The multilevel reading of the book helps to provide an account of the plasticity of creating a teacher community for professional development within the group, the community, and the network.

The book invites the reader to complex learning design that combines things, tasks, and people in a group, community, and network. As proposed by Goodyear, Carvalho, and Dohn (2014), we recognize the danger of this approach: "If everything is connected to everything else, then where does one begin? How does one avoid an exponential growth in interdependencies?" (p. 143).

Our solution points to multilevel design based on and oriented to the creation of a lived learning experience. This means sustaining a space of actions and possibilities validated by actual configurations and workable conditions. With this in mind, the very concept of *learning environments* extends beyond the presence of online and hybrid solutions. The learning space thus becomes the whole material, affective, and social context in which the group, community, and network are imagined and experienced.

**Table I.1. Map of the Book**

| | To Know | | | To Think | |
|---|---|---|---|---|---|
| | Prospective | | Concept | Technology | Metaphor |
| How | Group | Community | Network | Interprofessionalism | Social Networks | Square |
| Entering | Belonging | Participation | Fluidity | Identity-Based Learning | Avatar and Cyborg | Virus |
| Socializing | Behaviors | Practice | Connection | Personal Meaning Making | Robotics | Boundaries |
| Developing | Growth | Cycle | Translation | Susurration | Hybrid and Augmented | Holobiont |
| Connecting | Resources | Repertoire | Lines | Extended Cognition | Artificial Intelligence | Rhizome |
| Expanding | Status | Engagement | Multi-expertise | Externality | GPS | Knots |
| Move On | Exit | Transformation | Disconnection | Diffractive Learning | Online Application | Graft |

Table I.2. Applications for Learning Design

| | |
|---|---|
| How | Self-Regulated Learning |
| Entering | Collaborative Scripts |
| Socializing | Role Taking and Feedback |
| Developing | Trialogical Learning |
| Connecting | Virtual Exchange |
| Expanding | Zone of Possibility |
| Move On | Affectivity in Learning |

We wish the readers their *signature pedagogies*—critical aspects to think, perform, and act with integrity the three fundamental dimensions of professional work (Shulman, 2005)—to improve in and through teacher collectives.

## REFERENCES

Caena, F., & Redecker, C. (2019). Aligning teacher competence frameworks to 21st-century challenges: The case for the European digital competence framework for educators (Digcompedu). *European Journal of Education, 54*(3), 356–369.

Goodyear, P., Carvalho, L., & Dohn, N. (2014). Design for networked learning: Framing relations between participants' activities and the physical setting. In S. Bayne, C. Jones, M. de Laat, T. Ryberg, & C. Sinclair (Eds.), *Proceedings of the 9th International Conference on Networked Learning* (pp. 137–144). University of Edinburgh.

Morris, S. M., & Stommel, J. (2018). *An urgency of teachers: The work of critical digital pedagogy*. Hybrid Pedagogy.

Shulman, L. S. (2005). Signature pedagogies in the professions. *Daedalus, 134*(3), 52–59.

*Part I*

*Chapter One*

# Creating a Teacher Collective

I am a social relation of me to myself. —L. S. Vygotsky (1989)

In educational literature, we observe the emergence of the concept of teacher collectives to resolve educational, managerial, or research-related problems. But what does it mean to create a collective of teachers? What are the theoretical viewpoints from which to start before considering the creation of a teacher collective?

This section briefly outlines three critical perspectives related to the theme of teacher collectives, allowing a broad overview of the possible theoretical and practical avenues.

## THREE PERSPECTIVES OF A TEACHER COLLECTIVE

This chapter discusses the creation of teacher collectives for learning and professional development. As a theoretical reference, the section introduces three central perspectives about the collective: the *group*, *community*, and *network*. Each of these will be described by referring to some essential readings and their authors.

### Group

Groups are a central topic in learning and teaching practices. In the dictionary definition, we find different meanings of the term group, including "a group of people united by natural bonds, relationships of interest, common goals and ideas." This definition does not help us fully understand the complexity of individual and group relationships. In Plato's *Republic* and Aristotle's *Poli-*

*tics*, there are reflections on collective phenomena, the structures that sustain life, and the relationships that regulate life in the polis.

In the classical psychology literature, individuals and society often are considered two separate and autonomous concepts. The individual is a being who exists entirely for himself or herself, and society is a reality that inexplicably exists beyond the individual. McGrath (1984, p. 12) states that, although it is true that each group is an aggregation of individuals, each aggregation of individuals does not necessarily become a group. The author distinguishes between:

- Artificial aggregations (e.g., individuals included in the same group for statistical purposes).
- Unorganized aggregates: people in the same place or situation, such as those sharing physical proximity or the same travel destination.
- Social units with relationship models (e.g., fans of the same team and young people with the same passion for a musical genre).
- Structured social units (e.g., groups of people attending the same gym or party).
- Intentionally designed social units (e.g., sports organizations, federations, sports teams, or work groups).
- Less intentionally designed social units, such as voluntary sports organizations.

As can be easily understood, no category is exclusive.

Earlier on, Bales (1950) distinguished between instrumental behavior (i.e., directed to the realization of a task) and socio-emotional or expressive behavior (manifestation of positive feelings and emotions, such as joking, praising, and helping). These categories generally are activated during all group activities. If problems threatening group stability arise during the instrumental activity, these tensions are attenuated by neutralization processes made possible by expressive activities.

We can also distinguish between large groups ("extended" groups), with a vast number of members, and small groups ("restricted" groups), with a limited number of members.

In the literature, we also find further categorizations of groups such as primary groups (who interact directly, linked by emotional bonds) and secondary groups (who interact directly or indirectly), formal groups based on the decision to constitute a group or informal groups that are spontaneous or natural aggregations formed not to pursue a purpose but based on the intensity of relationships (e.g., groups of adolescents).

Finally, in the literature, it is also possible to find many other typologies of the group—for example, natural groups that exist independent of research activities and purposes; artificial groups that are created exclusively for research purposes; reference groups, understood as groups with which individuals identify themselves or to which individuals aspire to belong. All of these classifications demonstrate the complexity of the relationship between individuals and groups.

The revival of the interest in groups only started in 1990 under the influence of the theories of Tajfel (1981), Moscovici (1984), and Turner (1987), central authors in outlining the study of the interaction between an individual and a group.

The symbol of the first phase is the text *The Crowd: A Study of the Popular Mind* by Gustave Le Bon (1895), who was the first to scientifically study the behavior of crowds, trying to identify their peculiar character and proposing suitable techniques to guide and control the masses. Le Bon's perspective is attributable to the "theory of contagion" based on the idea of mental contagion to explain collective behavior that deviates from personal logic.

The studies on active minorities conducted by Serge Moscovici and Willem Doise at the end of the 1960s show how minority groups (i.e., groups that do not conform to the rules imposed by the majority) can trigger significant social change processes.

The second phase of interest in the group proposes a more positive vision of the man-group relationship. Below, we briefly present the four main theories about the group in social psychology: those of Kurt Lewin, Muzafer Sherif, Henri Tajfel, and John Turner.

## Kurt Lewin

The centrality of groups in the processes of social change is affirmed by Kurt Lewin (1890–1947), one of the prominent founding fathers of the psychology of groups. He developed the "field theory" model, which explains behavior according to the situation in which it occurs, influenced by a Gestalt approach.

Inspired by the model of electromagnetism developed by physicist James Klerk Maxwell (1864), Lewin graphically represented "the field" as an area divided into different regions, delimited by borders but simultaneously communicating and dependent on each other. Inside, a dynamic relationship is determined by forces (expressed with a vector indicating direction and intensity) and valences (the value a region acquires at a particular moment for the person).

Lewin also used the force field metaphor to understand groups: just as the individual and his environment form a psychological field, the group and its environment form a social field. The person forms a unitary interacting totality, within which every change involves a rearrangement of the whole field. The field can have many degrees of differentiation, depending on the person's experiences. This field consists of:

- Living space: the subjective psychological representation that the person has of the environment.
- Social and environmental facts: what happens in the physical and social world without temporarily affecting the individual's living space.
- Border area: representing the border between objectivity and subjectivity, where the space of life and the outside world meet.

Fundamental is the concept of interdependence, which highlights how an individual's experiences, actions, and results are closely linked to those of the other group members. The interdependence of the task can be positive or negative: in the first case, collaboration and success of the whole group are achieved; in the second, however, there is competition, and the success of one member is obtained at the expense of the others.

Both types of interdependence create dynamics that affect group productivity and internal climate. Dewey and Lewin contributed to the diffusion of lines of thought to enhance cooperative learning in school.

According to Lewin, groups can be mediators of social change. This claim is supported by the "discovery" in 1946 of the Training Group (T-group). The T-group is a learning experience through which participants acquire a greater sensitivity to group phenomena and a more accurate perception of themselves and others. Lewin observed that giving feedback to the group participants on their way of interacting and their attitudes makes learning more effective, refining their perception of themselves and others.

The T-groups help stimulate change processes, both personal and social or organizational. According to Lewin, every person needs the group to define and express his or her identity. All groups have multiple aspects. Over time, the T-group has taken on various declinations and names with extensive applications in the clinical field.

Lewin was also responsible for the definition of action research (1946). Action research studies how change occurs and to what extent, the factors that can hinder it, what interventions to take if the intended change does not occur, as well as the effects of the intervention in the short and long term. This research methodology allows, on the one hand, intervention in social reality and, on the other hand, drawing new elements of knowledge from experiences in a dynamic relationship between theory and practice.

## Muzafer Sherif

A second founding father of social psychology is Sherif (1948). He considered the group as "a social unit consisting of a set of individuals who, at a given moment, are in a relationship of the mutual interdependence of status and role, and who, implicitly or explicitly, possess a defined set of norms and values capable of regulating the behavior of individual members" (1961, p. 10).

The temporal duration of internal relations discriminates between a group and a union. The first is marked by continuous interaction; the second, a short and transitory interrelation. In Sherif's structural conception, the central element is the repeated interaction between the members, which, over time, leads to the progressive specialization of the activities carried out in the group and the consequent diversification of roles, status, and power.

Sherif's definition is suitable for groups of various sizes and provides an interdisciplinary investigative approach between psychology, sociology, and anthropology.

Further, Sherif designed several studies to understand the modalities and dynamics between groups, demonstrating how the mere presence in the social context of an outgroup (i.e., a group outside its group) generates conflict between them.

## Henri Tajfel

The central scholar of group processes is Tajfel (1981). According to his theorization, a group exists when two or more individuals perceive themselves as members of the same social category: Tajfel proposed a group definition based on self-categorization and not, on the contrary, relegated to extrinsic events, historical, political, or economic aspects.

The author believed that it was possible to place all behavior along a continuum at the extremes of which we find interpersonal behavior (in which the interaction depends on individuals, personal characteristics, and interpersonal relationships) and intergroup behavior (where the business is determined by belonging to various groups). Social categorization causes intergroup behavior that discriminates against the "other" group and favors one's own, causing social behavior to shift between the two poles.

In his study of small and informal groups, Tajfel noted how it is sufficient to impose a criterion of social categorization from the outside, which distinguishes between a hypothetical in-group and an out-group, to develop behaviors favorable to the former and discriminatory toward the latter, thus speaking of a "model of minimal groups."

A central aspect of this theory is that belonging to the group is perceived not only by the person concerned but also through the recognition by the other members and by the consent given by the subjects not included: the agreement between internal and external criteria helps determine the behavior toward the in-group and the out-group.

According to Tajfel, this belonging to the group is at the same time cognitive (I recognize that I am part of a group), evaluative (I connote this consideration in a positive or negative sense), and emotional (the elaborated judgment is accompanied by feelings of pride, esteem, pleasure, regret, contempt, shame). Note how these characteristics of belonging apply to face-to-face interactions and relationships between broad social categories: intense affiliation is possible in small and macro-aggregative contexts.

Starting from these elaborations, Tajfel arrived at the formulation of the social identity theory (SIT), stating that each person's identity has a social component that comes from the experiences of belonging to different groups, combined with the emotional and value features of such membership.

## John Turner

Turner is a British social psychologist. In 1971 he enrolled at the University of Bristol to begin a doctoral dissertation under the supervision of Henri Tajfel.

According to Turner, the shift from interpersonal to intergroup behavior depends on changes in the functioning of the self-concept, which is made up of two elements (J. Turner et al., 1987): personal identity, made up of self-descriptions made based on individual characteristics; and social identity, composed of self-descriptions made based on group membership. In particular, the categorization proceeds using various levels of abstraction:

- Human identity: understood as the superordinate level of the self as a human being.
- Social identity: the intermediate level of the self as a member of a group in comparison to members of other groups.
- Personal identity: the subordinate level of the personal self: I evaluate myself as unique compared to the other in-group members, such as "I am a friendly person."

When individuals define themselves as members of a group, they create associations between themselves and the various attributes of the group they belong to, seeing themselves (and others) as interchangeable members of the same group.

Categorization is not constant but depends on context. This categorization and the theories referenced have influenced subsequent studies. For example, Donald Campbell (1958) introduced the concept of *entitativity*, in which an aggregate becomes an entity if its components are perceived as similar, close, and linked by a common destiny. Therefore, the entity is understood as the degree of reality, consistency, and homogeneity with which a group is perceived by individuals not belonging to it. This means that the psychological formation of a group originates among the members due to the multiplication of their common bonds.

In this chapter, we defined the group from the perspective of groups, briefly outlining the historical overview of the study of groups and the main theories by the founders of classical social psychology.

This second part of the chapter discusses the concept of "community," in particular, a community of practice.

## Community of Practice

The communities of practice (CoP) construct was developed by Jean Lave and Etienne Wenger (1991), who defined it as a group of people who share a topic or a passion for something they do and who regularly interact with learning how to do it better.

The concept's origins can be traced back to the situated learning theory (Lave, 1988; Brown et al., 1989). This approach considers cognition as a situated process. Learning is understood as an activity that takes place in the flow of experiences and not only within the individual's mind, becoming a process that acts in a socially and culturally defined manner: in this way, such theories "attribute primacy to the dynamics of everyday existence, to improvisation, coordination, and interactional choreography" (Wenger, 1998, p. 20).

A community of practice incorporates a long and diversified participation process, understood as a social and personal process.

The two processes of participation and reification are part of the negotiation processes: with participation, we project ourselves into the world; with reification, we attribute an autonomous existence to an object (like the passport that opens the passage through border gates). The two processes are distinct but complementary, forming a unity in their duality.

From these considerations, the concept of practice emerged as central (Brown & Duguid, 1991) and is understood as the actual realization of an activity, or rather "doing in a historical and social context that gives structure and meaning to our activity" (Wenger, 1998, p. 59), therefore a set of actions located in a context characterized by both artifacts and other individuals. This construct has been widely circulated in literature and is used in organizational, educational, and social fields of study.

According to Wenger (1998), CoPs are "an integral part of our daily life. They are so informal and so pervasive that they rarely enter the crosshairs of detailed analysis" (p. 14). For the author, three conditions allow the practice to be carried out within a community, triggering processes of negotiation of meaning: mutual commitment, joint enterprise, and shared repertoire.

Belonging to a community is a *mutual commitment* because the individual's work is essential for achieving the common goal. The mutual commitment of its members allows the creation of products, services, and, in general, the execution of a task or function. What makes this mutual commitment possible implies diversity and homogeneity: in the example that Wenger (1998) proposed, the group comprises heterogeneous people by training and aspiration (women with children, part-time students, etc.). However, their relationships are linked through the shared commitment to managing the insurance reimbursements they carry out in the company. Mutual commitment also implies an awareness of one's competence and that of others (e.g., in a surgical team, mutual commitment implies complementary contributions) but can also involve overlapping forms of competence (as in the example of liquidators, where several employees have the same duties).

Mutual commitment does not involve total and constant homogeneity. Still, it is based on functional relationships, so in a CoP, in addition to peaceful coexistence relationships, dissensions, tensions, and conflicts are also possible: these forms of "dissent, challenge, and competition can become legitimate forms of participation" (Wenger, 1998, p. 92).

The creation of mutual commitment does not occur only through various elements (such as working in the same place and carrying out the exact same tasks in the same hours) but also through participation in informal processes within the community (such as sharing and telling personal stories during coffee breaks).

*The shared practice* implies heterogeneous and complex modalities, which reflect the complexity of interactions between people. Each group member's work implies an interdependence with the work of other members, where each participant fills a unique place and develops an exclusive identity that is defined and integrated into his or her participation. In general, developing mutual commitment requires negotiating and connecting different perspectives, interests, and aspirations. For Wenger, mutual commitment consists of three mechanisms:

1. cooperative work: working together for the realization of the same product or service;

2. diversity and partiality: complementarity in working methods and opinions that enrich the process of achieving the common goal; and
3. mutual functional relationships: characterized by positive emotions but also by dysfunctional relationships between members of the community aimed at negotiating and connecting perspectives.

The collective negotiation process makes it possible to create a *joint enterprise*, which is therefore not based on a prior agreement between all members nor equality of ideas but is achieved through the coordination of different perspectives. The joint enterprise holds together a community of practice and polarizes its activity. Co-constructed through discursive interactions in the development of practices, it constitutes the sense of the community and its raison d'être: "A joint enterprise is a process, not a static agreement.... An enterprise is a resource of coordination, of sense-making, of mutual engagement" (Wenger, 1998, p. 82).

The effective conduct of the activity requires that individuals feel involved in the joint venture, and each member of the community recognizes the others' tasks as relevant. Communities of practice are not independent but develop within historical, social, cultural, and institutional contexts. Finally, Wenger emphasizes mutual accountability as the element that makes it possible to distinguish what is salient within a CoP:

> This regime of mutual accountability plays a central role in defining the circumstances in which, as a community and as individuals, members feel more or less concerned about what they do and what happens to them and around them and in which they try to avoid or refuse to make sense of events and to seek new meanings. (Wenger, 1998, p. 97)

*The shared repertoire* comprises habits, languages, codes, specialized terms, beliefs, rituals, and memories that reflect the stories and expectations. The elements that make up this repertoire are not heterogeneous but acquire consistency because they belong to the same practice and are helpful for the continuation of the same business. Through references to a shared canon, the community members have the opportunity to communicate, identifying structures that are useful for mutual understanding.

Communities are incessantly engaged in negotiating meaning precisely to build and expand their shared repertoire, allowing innovation and creating increasingly complex forms of activity (Wenger, 1998). The shared repertoire has an open character and leaves room for ambiguity, making it possible to generate and negate new meanings in interaction: stories, for example, create common points of reference among the members and become a resource for creating different stories.

Such ambiguity requires a continuous effort to clarify the quality and transparency of communication, making communication unpredictable and dynamic (such as metaphors in a speech).

These three dimensions are not constituted through formal teaching and learning but in the informal social interactions between the members of the CoP.

## Network

To talk about networks, we use the actor-network theory (ANT) (Callon, 1986; Callon & Latour, 1981; Latour, 1986; Law, 1992). Law (1992) describes the central proposition of ANT:

> This, then, is the core of the actor-network approach: a concern with how actors and organisations mobilize, juxtapose, and hold together the bits and pieces out of which they are composed; how they are sometimes able to prevent those bits and pieces from following their inclinations and making off; and how they manage. As the above quotation suggests, the basic idea of ANT is to understand how actors—both human and non-human—are brought together in stable, heterogeneous networks of aligned interests.
>
> By tracing the transformation of these heterogeneous networks, ANT explores how these networks of actors, and their relations emerge, are maintained, and compete with other networks of aligned interests. As a result, to conceal for a time the process of translation itself and turn a network from a heterogeneous set of bits and pieces, each with its inclinations, into something that passes as a punctuated actor. (p. 386)

Three main principles underlie the ANT approach: generalized symmetry, agnosticism, and free association (Callon, 1986).

First, the principle of *generalized symmetry* is reflected in the definition of actors—in which no distinction between human and nonhuman actors is made. Both should be analyzed in the same terms without discrimination, starting from the idea that both human and nonhuman actors can take action.

Second, the principle of *agnosticism* suggests that the observer of the actor network needs to be impartial and requires that all interpretations be unprivileged. This principle requires researchers to avoid censoring any interpretation provided by the actors systematically studied when they speak about themselves or other actors (Callon, 1986), even when their interpretations fail to accord with the researcher's views (Law, 1986). Censoring interpretations potentially can hinder an in-depth understanding of the phenomenon under investigation.

Third, the principle of *free association* requires abandoning all a priori relationships that could be assumed to exist between human and nonhuman actors (Callon, 1986). The actors' relationships and how they explain their worlds must fluctuate in any analysis. Rather than imposing these relationships upon the actors, they must focus on the analysis, not the point of departure (1986, p. 201).

Whereas actors are individual entities, actor networks (or only networks) are actors: networks are composed of heterogeneous materials linked through different relationships and overcome resistance (Law, 1992). For a new network to emerge, the controlling actor—and those exercising control on its behalf—needs to enroll some actors to align their interests and weaken others who might act against the network's goals. Once the controlling actor has translated the interests of others to achieve the aims, the actor network is stabilized.

The process of simplifying networks is known as "punctualization," an actor network that can be seen as a single and coherent actor with relatively few apparent parts. Once unactualized, an actor network can be taken for granted, no longer questioned or tested: it becomes "a black box whose behavior is known and predicted independently of its context" (Callon, 1991, p. 152). The "black-boxing" process is open enough to make it possible for the sub-networks to disappear and actor networks to become actors.

The process of punctualization is always precarious. The actor network always has the potential to change and evolve because the relationships linking the actors of the network may be weakened or because other actors external to the actor network can threaten its stability. Only when a network is formed of a range of durable materials can it be seen as relatively stable (Law, 1992, p. 387).

The presentation of the three concepts of group, community, and network refers to three different approaches: a more static one, typical of classical psychology, with identifiable and reconstructible dynamics; a situated and dynamic approach, where the process of negotiation and construction of meaning dominates; and, finally, an approach more in tune with a postmodern vision, where the human and the nonhuman begin to mirror themselves in a balanced way.

Although the three perspectives emerged chronologically later as a development field, they can be traced to the actuality of the collectives organized in educational interventions. In teacher training, the three approaches can inspire differentiated planning of collective interventions. Creating a collective of teachers can therefore mean positioning oneself on one of the three perspectives to subsequently probe its implementation and development.

The potential of the collective organized as a group, community, or network is central in a society where there is the need to work together with other actors in a multi- and interdisciplinary way.

## One Concept, One Technology, and One Metaphor
*Interprofessional Collaboration, Social Networks, and Square*

The ability to work interprofessionally is not an explicitly developed competence in teacher training. A teacher's work becomes increasingly interdisciplinary: the teacher has always worked at the interface of various other roles (such as that of a relative) and colleagues with different roles—school administrative staff, representatives of institutions, and researchers (Impedovo, 2021). Several projects have been conceived to develop perspectives and practices of communication, sharing, and understanding between different members and teams (for a reference, see Arànega, 2018, about the Spanish context).

Interprofessional competencies make it possible to nourish professional practices through interaction with others (Colinet, 2011). The main framework has six areas according to a Canadian model called the Canadian Interprofessional Health Collaborative (2010): care centered on the person, communication, clarification of roles, teamwork, collaborative leadership, and interprofessional conflict resolution.

Interprofessional competence makes it possible to promote professional identity development (Clairet, 2013), promote students from each profession getting together (Renaut et al., 2015), and make them want to work in an interprofessional setting later. It prepares students to meet multifactorial societal needs in practice settings (Fonds de recherche du Québec [FRQ], 2020) and promotes the professional integration of students by increasing their sense of competence (Mukamurera, 2018).

Interprofessional collaboration could facilitate taking different positions, helping reframe constraints in new ways, and enriching understanding and mutual commitment. Sharing can be superficial and oriented to exchanging information and resources or more engaged in reflexive practices, social presence, and critical engagement to generate new knowledge. The participatory nature of the community could facilitate forms of so-called *relational agency* (Edwards, 2017), which involves the use of knowledge to take engaged action with others.

At the same time, interprofessional collaboration can also be a space of tension and frustration among professionals. Joining in an interprofessional discussion means engaging in an articulated conversation where professionals are explicitly committed to seeking mutual understanding but not necessarily agreement. Indeed, all participants are invited to recognize their interests in the problem as necessary, even if they disagree on how to address it. For example, an organization could provide a physical or online space in which one community member can freely decide to join (or not) the discussion, explicitly recognizing the possible divergent opinions that may arise.

Technology, like social networks (Vangrieken et al., 2017), strengthens the potentiality of collaboration. The main advantages of social media for learning are sharing resources and ideas, facilitating knowledge exchange, and cultivating different forms of solid or weak relationships. Social networks such as Twitter, Facebook, Instagram, and Snapchat are widely used (Digital Report, 2020). For example, social networks such as Facebook, which were primarily conceived for socialization, have now become oriented toward professional use—a phenomenon called professional Facebooking. Social networking makes possible a networked community of practice (Wenger-Traynor et al., 2015), which stresses the centrality of the relationships, personal interactions, and connections oriented to sharing information and helpful resources, and contributing to individuals' collective professional development.

The image that we can associate with this overview is that of the town or city square: let us think about the role of the square in small Italian cities, around which cities are built and organized, or the big Shibuya Crossing in Tokyo. The square helps connect the concepts developed in this chapter. Social networks are the modern square, an image already likely present in collectives (such as the WhatsApp groups on our phones). People transit, stay briefly or for a longer time, discuss, move on, and engage with others, in a society or in a structured or unstructured event to contribute to or observe the ongoing social dynamic.

Inviting teachers into a group, community, or network means letting them enjoy a meaningful space of potential learning and caring interactions. Everyone's direct or indirect contributions are already embedded in the square's design: without borders, accessible, and open. The square allows everyone to be hosted in the role that a single individual or group prefers. All members can contribute, give something, or not, to the collective—a song, a performance, a chat, a smile. The square becomes a space of narration of the collective life.

## For Learning Design

*Face-to-Face, Blended, and Hybrid*

Knowing how to deal with a collective is attractive, especially if it is face-to-face or online in a blended or hybrid modality.

When a teacher or student teacher joins a community through an online, blended, or hybrid modality, this implies a complex activity that the teacher or student teacher is called to carry out progressively, and more and more autonomously during their practice or training. The term "self-regulation" generally indicates the regulation of a process, a plant, or an agent that adapts to reality. In education, self-regulated learning (SRL) refers to the transversal competence of "learning to learn" that allows one to activate and maintain cognitions and behaviors constantly oriented toward learning objectives. In an educational context, improving self-learning requires personalizing the learning needs of individual learners, motivating them to take greater responsibility for what and how to learn, or as Zeidner and colleagues stated it:

> Self-regulation involves cognitive, affective, motivational and behavioral components that give the individual the capacity to adjust their actions and goals to achieve the desired results in light of changing environmental conditions. (Zeidner et al., 2000, p. 751)

This definition proposes SRL as the ability to autonomously control one's learning process at a cognitive, metacognitive, and behavioral level, as well as maintaining adequate motivation and effective management of one's emotions, fostering awareness of one's path and mistakes. Without these skills, a student cannot take an active and autonomous part in the learning process and make the most of contexts and resources, regardless of the training model that the teacher proposes. Therefore, self-regulation strategies can be multiple and, above all, actively learned.

Creating a community and making available theoretical resources and tools for self-diagnostic of main features, attitudes, skills, and competencies has become a way to let students explore new modalities of learning regulation. Today, different learning environments share open educational resources (OER) that can be easily aggregated and shared. Indeed, it is essential to reference concepts not yet explored by the learners to open new gates of awareness and understanding.

## TAKEAWAY IDEAS FROM THIS CHAPTER

### Reflecting on Observed Social Interactions and Social Space

In this section, you will create your own takeaway ideas from the chapter, because we think that the best takeaways are the ones that you construct on your own. You are the one who knows most about your context. Rather than giving you a to-do list, we feel that it will be much more meaningful and fruitful for you to construct your own takeaways. In a way, you are conducting a case study using your experiences. Therefore, at the end of each chapter, you will see a takeaway section that includes a series of questions to guide you to reflect on your experiences and construct your takeaways.

Educational practice is highly dependent on the nature of social interactions that take place in the school community and beyond. Regarding this practice and social interactions, numerous theories exist in education and social sciences, but one important issue we should deal with is overcoming the theory and practice gap. Applying academic educational theories to an educational practice does not necessarily guarantee improved quality of practice because educational practice is embedded in a social and cultural context. It is not free from economic, legal, and political dynamics, and it cannot be modeled by a finite set of academic theories. Therefore, academic theories that assume to describe "universal truths" cannot serve as a magic wand in real-life practices.

But academic theories are not totally useless. Academic educational theories can be used as guides to consider new directions of professional practice in your context. What we recommend is that you go back and forth between what academic theories suggest and what you perceive to be the needs of your contextual environment, then engage in reflective inquiries to consider how to transform your professional practice in the process. This is how the takeaway section is structured in each chapter.

In this chapter, we discussed key theories related to the creation of a teacher collective. Below are a series of guiding questions for you to think about this issue. Reflect on your experiences and jot down your answers, even if they are only rough ideas. These notes will serve as your personal takeaways from this chapter.

- Surely many social interactions are taking place among teachers at your school. Observe your surroundings and see how people are interacting with each other. How are your colleagues communicating with each other: in person or online? What seems to be the nature of the ways people (including you) communicate with each other? And how do some people choose, or not, to communicate with others? What does it tell you about the nature of teacher collectives in your workplace?
- Consider social interactions among colleagues that seem to be contributing to professional development of your community members. Suppose that you heard informal conversations in your school's corridors where your colleagues engaged in problem solving on new curriculum implementation. Then you saw another pair of colleagues engaging in a different kind of conversation, but they joined the conversation of the former pair. Then

the two pairs co-discovered the common source of the issues that can "kill two birds with one stone." Or you may not see this kind of conversation at all as people tend to focus on their individual work at your workplace. What do you see as the pattern that characterizes the social interactions among your colleagues? What does it tell you about the nature of teacher collectives in your workplace?
- Think about how you communicated with your colleagues in your school community over the past few weeks. Why did you choose to communicate with some colleagues but not others? How did you communicate with them, and what did you learn from the interactions? What does it tell you about where you are in the professional community?
- How do you think the physical environment in your school shapes the nature of social interactions among your colleagues? Could there be more appropriate settings that might get people better connected and promote active exchange of ideas?
- How could different kinds of technology play a role there? How easy or difficult is it to use digital space and online exchanges for the purpose? How could the digital space and the physical space interact with each other? What can be done to improve this situation for the development of a teacher collective?
- What kinds of groups do you think exist in your workplace? To which group do you belong? What does it mean to be in the group? For example, groups might be united based on a certain value system, role in the workplace, age, gender, ethnicity, and so forth. How are they formed? How is technology playing a role in forming and reforming new groups?
- Almost every industry needs to support the development of its professionals. What do you think of the idea of expanding your professional network to interact with those who are outside education using technology, online space, and more so that you can initiate interdisciplinary dialogues?
- Have you already established mutually beneficial relationships with people in professions outside education? If so, what have you learned from them? How is it possible for you to increase such opportunities?
- As a social space, how open or closed is your workplace to newcomers or outsiders? If it is closed, what actions do you think need to be initiated to promote collaborative dialogues and co-reflections beyond the border?

## REFERENCES

Arànega, S. (2018). *El trabajo en equipo interdisciplinar en la universidad con estudiantes de diferentes titulaciones del ámbito educativo.* Editorial Octaedro.

Bales, R. F. (1950). *Interaction process analysis: A method for the study of small groups.* Addison-Wesley.

Brown, J. S., Collins, A., & Duguid, P. (1989, January–February). Situated cognition and the culture of learning. *Educational Researcher 18*(1), 32–41.

Brown, J. S., & Duguid, P. (1991). Organizational learning and communities-of-practice: Toward a unified view of working, learning, and innovation. *Organization Science, 2*(1), 40–57. https://doi.org/10.1287/orsc.2.1.40

Callon, M. (1986). Some elements of a sociology of translation: Domestication of the scallops and the fishermen of St Brieuc Bay. In J. Law (Ed.), *Power, action and belief: A new sociology of knowledge?* (pp. 196–229). Routledge and Kegan Paul.

Callon, M. (1991). Techno-economic networks and irreversibility. In J. Law (Ed.), *A sociology of monsters: Essays on power, technology and domination* (pp. 132–165). Routledge.

Callon, M., & Latour, B. (1981). Unscrewing the big Leviathan: How actors macro-structure reality and how sociologists help them to do so. In K. D. Knorr-Cetina & A.V. Cocourel (Eds.), *Advances in social theory and methodology: Toward an integration of micro and macro-sociologies* (pp. 277–303). Routledge and Kegan Paul.

Campbell, D. T. (1958). Common fate, similarity, and other indices of the status of aggregates of a person as social entities. *Behavioural Science, 3*, 14–25.

Canadian Interprofessional Health Collaborative. (2010). *A national interprofessional competency framework.* Canadian Interprofessional Health Collaborative. https://phabc.org/wp-content/uploads/2015/07/CIHC-National-Interprofessional-Competency-Framework.pdf

Clairet, L. (2013). *Le développement de l'identité professionnelle des futurs travailleurs sociaux à travers la formation universitaire de premier cycle* (Doctoral dissertation, Université du Québec en Outaouais).

Colinet, S. (2011). La formation des enseignants par la mutualisation des pratiques avec les professionnels des services sociaux. *La nouvelle revue de l'adaptation et de la scolarisation, 3*, 215–227.

Digital Report. (2020). https://wearesocial.com/digital-2020

Edwards, A. (Ed.). (2017). *Working relationally in and across practices: A cultural-historical approach to collaboration.* Cambridge University Press.

Fonds de recherche du Québec (FRQ). (2020). https://frq.gouv.qc.ca

Impedovo, M. A. (2021). Teacher-researcher collaborations: Negotiations of research practices in school. *Transformative Dialogues: Teaching and Learning Journal, 14*(2).

Latour, B. (1986). The powers of association. In J. Law (Ed.), *Power, action and belief: A new sociology of knowledge?* (pp. 264–280). Routledge and Kegan Paul.

Lave, J. (1988). *Cognition in practice.* Cambridge University Press.

Lave, J., & Wenger, E. (1991). *Situated learning: Legitimate peripheral participation.* Cambridge University Press.

Law, J. (1986). The heterogeneity of texts. In M. Callon, J. Law, & A. Rip (Eds.), *Mapping the dynamic of science and technology: Sociology of science in the real world* (pp. 67–83). Macmillan.

Law, J. (1992). Notes on the actor-network theory: Ordering, strategy, and heterogeneity. *Systems Practice, 5*(4), 379–393.
Le Bon, G. (1895, trans. 1947). *The crowd: A study of the popular mind*. Ernest.
Lewin, K. (1946). Action research and minority problems. *Journal of Social Issues, 2*, 34–46.
Maxwell, J. K. (1864). *A dynamical theory of the electromagnetic field*. Scozia.
McGrath, J. E. (1984). *Groups: Interaction and performance*. Prentice-Hall.
Moscovici, S. (1984). The phenomenon of social representations. In R. Farr & S. Mascovici, (Eds.), *Social representations* (pp. 3–70). Cambridge University Press.
Mukamurera, J. (2018). Les préoccupations, le sentiment de compétence et les besoins de soutien professionnels des enseignants débutants: Un état de la situation au Québec. In J. Mukamurera, J.-F. Desbiens, & T. Perez-Roux (Eds.), *Se développer comme professionnel dans les occupations adressées à autrui: Conditions, modalités et perspectives* (pp. 189–237). Montréal, Québec. Les éditions JFD.
Renaut, P., Fiquet, L., Allory, E., Chapron, A., Hugé, S., & Annezo, F. (2015). Le speed dating pédagogique: Une innovation pour enseigner la collaboration interprofessionnelle. https://www.researchgate.net/publication/285338053_Le_speed _dating_pedagogique_une_innovation_pour_enseigner_la_collaboration_interpro fessionnelle_Renaut_P_Fiquet_L_All ory_E_Chapron_A_Huge_S_Annezo_F
Sherif, M. (1948). *An outline of social psychology*. Harper.
Sherif, M., Harvey, O. J., White, B. J., Hood, W. R., & Sherif, C. (1961). *Intergroup cooperation and conflict: The robbers cave experiment*. University of Oklahoma Press.
Tajfel, H. (1981). *Human groups and social categories*. Cambridge University Press.
Turner, J. C., Hogg, M. A., Oakes, P. J., Reicher, S. D., & Wetherell, M. S. (1987). *Rediscovering the social group: A self-categorization theory*. Basil Blackwell.
Turner, V. (1987). *The anthropology of performance*. PAJ Publications.
Vangrieken, K., Meredith, C., Packer, T., & Kyndt, E. (2017). Teacher communities as a context for professional development: A systematic review. *Teaching and Teacher Education, 61*, 47–59.
Vygotsky L. S. (1989). Concrete human psychology. *Soviet Psychology, 27*(2), 53–77.
Wenger, E. (1998). *Communities of practice: Learning, meaning and identity*. Cambridge University Press.
Wenger-Trayner, E., Fenton-O'Creevy, H. S., Kubiak, C., & Wenger-Traynor, B. (2015). *Learning in landscapes of practice: Boundaries, identity and knowledgeability*. Practice-Based Learning.
Zeidner, M., Boekaerts, M., & Pintrich, P. R. (2000). Self-regulation: Directions and challenges for future research. In M. Boekaerts, P. R. Pintrich, & M. Zeider (Eds.), *Handbook of self-regulation* (pp. 749–768). Academic Press.

*Chapter Two*

# Entering into a Teacher Collective

When we go online, our feet are still on the ground. —N. K. Hayles (2000)

Entering a collective could be a learning experience for teachers. Traditionally, a teacher is alone in the classroom, in the presence of students. After the lesson, teachers go to a space in the school where they can have coffee, meet colleagues, prepare instructional materials, and obtain information about teachers' unions, rights, initiatives, and so forth. A real confrontation of practices between teachers is a new phenomenon, supported by research and critical initiatives to implement individual and collective transformation.

COVID-19 has introduced different disruptions inside and outside the classroom: new educational technologies, pedagogical methodologies, and collective experiences. In this crisis, the general society discovered teachers' unique role: teachers are now fully recognized as the "glue" between contexts (home and school), curriculum content, local expertise, situational zones of development, and social and emotional regulation. The teacher is still in the classroom, but the classroom is open to the world through technology, social implications, and parents and society observing what goes on inside the classroom.

The teacher image has become new and different in the eyes of society; at the same time, the role of the teacher is internally complete and unchanged: teachers experience stress due to various constraints, low salaries in different contexts, and missed opportunities for authentic lifelong learning. For these reasons, the collective is a possible solution for sharing content, pedagogies, technological literacy, and developing professional experiences for individual and collective growth.

## THREE PERSPECTIVES

Joining a new collective, a new community, is a complex experience, that goes hand in hand with acquiring cultural references and managing new information. The experience of entering a new collective is also an emotional experience. Usually, the integration process into a new collective involves a phase of transition that can lead to some form of change, both in the collective and in the single participant. Here, three perspectives are related to entry into the collective: belonging, participation, and fluidity.

## Belonging

In an anthropological reading, entering a group has various personal and social implications. The anthropologist Arnold van Gennep (1909) first used the term "rites of passage," defined as a series of acts and ceremonies by which a new member is admitted to participating in a group from which some are excluded. The ceremonies are intended as the rules that society produces to maintain balance, allowing the cohesion and continuity of the group's heritage of values and experiences. The author distinguishes three types of rites based on the function they perform:

1. separation or "liminary" rites, which act at the moment of detachment or abandonment of the previous state;
2. marginal or "liminary" rites, understood as a moment of suspension, in which those involved in the rite find themselves in a condition of liminality (or ambiguity). The margin is a "moment" of transit, characterized by the absence of a clear definition of the role of the subjects involved: it relegates the individual to the margins of society while awaiting his or her entry into a new social status;
3. rites of aggregation or "postliminary" facilitate readmission into society under the new condition.

Van Gennep also underlined how a change in social status (birth, initiation, marriage, death) involves, in addition to the subject performing the rite, even other community subjects. The rite, therefore, fulfills two functions: for the individual, it changes social identity and stimulates greater loyalty; for the group, it strengthens borders.

In addition to the rites of passage, the entry of a new member into the group is identified as "initiation."

The rites of passage do not only belong to the so-called primitive cultures; we also find them in our everyday life, with different dynamics and meanings: the most ancestral part of us still needs symbols and ceremonies (such as piercing, tattoos, "welcome" ceremonies celebrated for new employees in work environments).

Lewin (1951) used the expression "social locomotions" to indicate the transitions from one social group to another or the movements and transactions that a person makes through a (professional) field (e.g., approaching or moving away from the goal). Moreland and Levine (1989) specify four tactics that make it easier for novices to join the group:

1. Conduct an effective recognition process during the exploration phase. In this phase, the novice evaluates and establishes whether the group is adequate to meet his or her needs without being satisfied with vague and approximate information.
2. Playing the role of the "new member": the novice should meet the group's expectations, showing dependence on the old times and conformity with the group's norms. Such behaviors increase the likelihood of being accepted by senior members and receiving more information and sharing to be effectively integrated into the group.
3. Look for trusted contacts: identify a figure among the "old-timers" who will help the newcomer become a full group member. Playing the role of tutor or mentor, the senior member will try to facilitate socialization due to a close relationship.
4. Collaborating with the other novices allows easier socialization, given the joint effort to assimilate and integrate into the new group. Moreover, if dissatisfied, they will work together to request the necessary accommodation from the group to be accepted.

Entry into the group is, therefore, characterized as a moment of negotiation between the individual and the group itself: for the novice, entry marks immersion in a real and specific group "culture," which includes knowledge, norms, traditions, routines (daily procedures), reports (members' stories), languages (group jargon or gestures understandable only by members), rituals (ceremonies or events), and symbols (objects with particular meaning).

The so-called negative initiations imply an "entry price" to pay. The entry cost stresses the transition to a new identity.

In another classic study in the school context, Zazzo (1984) identified remote observation as an adaptive behavior for a child who wants to fit into a new school group. Techniques considered unobtrusive for the entry of a new member into the group include wandering around, waiting, playing games, and making comments on the activities that senior group members carry out.

In today's social and educational contexts, interest is rising in the sentiment of belonging. The feeling of belonging is a complex process built gradually and in which the person must have enough energy to engage in a group. The need to belong is one of the most critical for all students to live well in all learning environments, including online (Peacock & Cowan, 2019).

A person must identify a group for which she has a real sense of belonging to make a positive contribution. The term "belonging" is used mainly to indicate an individual's affiliation with a group of people or communities, which can be defined based on specific social, cultural, legal, or territorial criteria. It can be a group, an association, a community, a socio-professional category, a class, or a social category.

In this first sense, the term belonging is used to indicate a condition of inclusion of an individual in a community or her recognition as a member of the latter. "Belonging" is also used to describe a feeling of identity, which expresses a cultural, ideological, or affective adherence to a community's unique and founding contents. To speak of belonging in this sense is to refer to this process of identification of individuals with the community to which they feel they belong. Identification involves recognizing oneself in the dominant and characteristic values, norms, lifestyles, and behaviors of a community (i.e., sharing its history and traditions, given that these distinctive traits or historico-cultural matrixes are socially recognized as such). Terminologies used are, for example, "school membership," "school belonging," "school connectedness," "sense of school membership," "sense of school belonging," or "youth connectedness." Goodenow (1993) defined a sense of belonging in this way: "Beyond appreciation or perceived warmth, it is also support and respect for personal autonomy and of the student as an individual" (p. 25).

Osterman (2010) believes that "[t]he reality is that students interpret good teaching as caring behavior" (p. 240). Several conditions are essential to accentuate young people's sense of belonging to an educational institution. The three main types of influence are the level of quality social interactions, effective pedagogy, and school organization facilitating the development of this feeling:

1. The feeling of belonging to the school and the quality of social relations, with the impression that the environment is meaningful, promote human contact.
2. Sense of belonging to the school and teaching practices/teacher support: the quality of pedagogy is essential to developing students' sense of belonging to a school. This includes the teaching system, supervision, recognition system, the quality of teaching, the time devoted to teaching, and opportunities for investment (Janosz et al., 1998).

3. The feeling of belonging to the school and school management: the actions of the administrators can aim to encourage more harmonious social relations and increase student participation in the life of the school.

Osterman (2010) identified pedagogical practices that foster a sense of belonging, such as high teacher expectations, relevant lessons, giving enough time to the student, emphasis on mastery of goals, frequent interactions to check student understanding, providing students with choices, varied activities, and availability of the teacher. Beyond this lies the dimension of caring as the belief of students that adults within their school community care about their learning, are interested in them as individuals, and have high academic expectations (Allen & Bowles, 2012).

A sense of belonging among higher education students is fundamental to their academic learning and success. Anderman and Freeman's model (2004) showed the determinants of school performance according to different groups of variables: some of these groups (the feeling of belonging, the expression of positive effects) present rather indirect links with school performance, whereas other groups of variables (the three types of student academic engagement) show direct (and proximal) links with students' mathematics performance.

Belonging to the institution can also lead to civic engagement (Gaskins et al., 2015).

## Participation

Wenger (1998) developed the concept of participation to refer to being part of a social community. The term participation etymologically refers to taking part in interpersonal relationships: in this meaning, participation refers to the social experience of living as a community member. Participation and constant interaction within the community develop a strong sense of belonging, as it implies sharing values, habits, and lifestyles. This allows the construction of the identity through the experiences of being involved.

Wenger (1998) distinguished four forms of participation: two are clear—full participation (consists in the active involvement of the participant) and full nonparticipation (consists in not being part of a community and, therefore, in exclusion from it); and two, peripherality and marginality, represent more subtle forms of nonparticipation. On the one hand, in the periphery, nonparticipation is understood as limited participation and constitutes an opportunity for learning, which allows for active involvement in the community, leading to full participation; marginality, on the other hand, prevents full participation and could lead to non-belonging because it consists of a condition of isolation.

The model of legitimated peripheral participation (Lave & Wenger, 1991) explains how it is possible to move from peripheral to more central participation for a neophyte who gradually learns to participate in community practices. This model considers knowledge acquisition progression from the periphery to the center of community activities. This path is intended as a gradual trajectory, conditioned by the specificity of the situation, which can hardly be established and predetermined a priori. The passage from the external and peripheral position toward the central position allows an individual member to become an expert in the specific practice of the community and, thus, become an influential member of the practice itself.

The novice can experience access to local resources during the process, developing increasingly complex and specific relational and procedural skills. According to Lave and Wenger (1991), learning as participation in a CoP is particularly effective when participants have:

- full access to different parts of the activity and progress over time toward broad participation in central tasks;
- sufficient horizontal interaction (between the participants), primarily mediated by stories of critical situations and their solutions; and
- transparent technologies and structures (i.e., their functioning is available and recurrent).

Hutchins (1995) speaks of the "horizon of observation" to emphasize the perspective available to the novice in participating in activities through different channels, such as written and verbal instructions, imitation or simple exposure to the behavior of others, and active sharing of work practices, interpretative models, and organizational customs and rituals of the community.

Central for newcomers is the socialization with experienced members of the same community, who act as "scaffolding" (Wood et al., 1976) elements between the demands of the task and the level of competence required. Interacting with expert colleagues teaches the newcomer to "see" social reality in a mediated way, favoring the understanding and coordination of tasks. Informal exchanges also allow the new member to discern between the relevant and irrelevant aspects of the profession. This process is beneficial when the novice recognizes the expert, who becomes a reference point.

The arrival of new members in a community is also a critical moment of change: "these generation meetings are the aspect of practice that is most often understood as learning" (Wenger, 1998, p. 117), which involves newcomers and already socialized members. As Wenger (1998) points out, "When neophytes enter the community, the generational discontinuities spread and expand within them; relationships change in a cascade process"

(p. 107): the members already inserted become elders, and the newcomers are helped to integrate.

Nonexpert colleagues also play an essential role in the insertion of the new members, motivating comparison and mutual exchange: socialization of knowledge allows the construction and sharing of solutions, the acquisition and use of specific terminology, mutual support, and the exchange of suggestions and ideas.

The centrality of the newcomer's learning path to community practices allows us to understand how knowledge and innovations circulate within the community. For example, some interesting studies were conducted by Goodwin (1994) about the "professional vision" of an archaeologist apprentice: professional discrimination occurs through an articulated visual, gestural, and verbal interaction between two archaeologists of different skills.

Orr (1990), on the community of repair technicians of Rank Xerox photocopiers, provided evidence about sharing stories, evocatively called "war stories," which is the privileged form chosen by the repairers to distribute professional competence among them.

Wenger (1998) defined three distinct modes of belonging: commitment, imagination, and alignment:

1. *Commitment* is understood as individuals' active and concrete involvement in the mutual negotiation processes of meaning. This commitment has a constrained character (for example, limits of time and space, physiological limits, etc.), which marks its strength and weakness: strength because it facilitates the negotiation process and weakness because it could lead to forms of self-referentiality, making the community of practice an obstacle to learning.
2. *Alignment* is the coordination of energies, actions, and practices to integrate into broader structures and contribute to larger enterprises: "through alignment, we become part of something big because we do what we need to play our role" (p. 203). Alignment amplifies our actions by coordinating different spaces, skills, and points of view within the community of practice. Alignment boosts power and possible meaning but can also be visionless and irresponsible if implemented with blind and uncritical obedience.
3. *Imagination* is understood as the creation of images of the world and the generation of new relationships in time and space, which become constitutive of the self because they expand commitment beyond certain constraints. To clarify this aspect, Wenger (1998, p. 175) relied on a story in which two stonemasons were asked what they were doing. One of the two, adhering to space-time constraints, replied, "I am cutting this stone to give it a square shape"; the other, however, expanding these boundaries, replied: "I am

building a cathedral." Both are doing the same thing, but their experiences and sense of self are profoundly different precisely because of imagination.

The image is, therefore, an essential component of our world experience and our sense of presence in it, with vast repercussions on identity: as Wenger (1998, p. 200) stated, "the concept of imagination refers to a process of expansion of our Self through the transcending of our time and space and the creation of new images of our world and ourselves." Moreover, it is not considered an individual and isolated event with personal fantasies; a way of belonging always involves social reality.

A complete definition of identity necessarily entails the experience of multi-membership that requires ongoing work of negotiation necessary to keep it "across boundaries," transversally to individual memberships. It is about negotiating identity across borders, discovering new ways, and effectively bringing together practices, methods of interaction, and responsibilities that lead back to different communities, representing diverse aspects of the self in distinct circumstances. The negotiation of identity aspects is possible, according to Wenger (2000), through a project with the following fundamental characteristics:

1. *Local coherence* is a peculiar experience of participation or nonparticipation in a specific community.
2. *Global extension*: a robust identity requires that members have lived rich and multiple experiences of participation in different communities and that the borders between the communities have been crossed.
3. *Social effectiveness*: a strong identity must allow participation in the social world with consequent enrichment of the individual's relational life.

Such a project is possible only through an ongoing process of comparison with others; identity is built only through the social dimension. As Wenger (2000) summarizes, the parallelism between practice and identity generates a perspective on identity that inherits the plot of practice. It follows that the identity, therefore, is:

- *lived*: identity is not an abstract category but an experience that involves participation and reification.
- *negotiated*: identity is becoming; it is a continuous and pervasive process.
- *social*: belonging to a community provides the identity with a predominantly social character.
- *learned*: identity is a trajectory over time that incorporates both the past and the future.

- *connected*: identity combines multiple forms of belonging through a reconciliation process that crosses the boundaries of practice.
- *interaction between local and global*: identity is shared between levels of experiences, close or far.

Using the terminology of distributed cognition, Hutchins (1995) talked about the social space in which knowledge is distributed among the interacting elements of the context, that is, people and artifacts.

Human cognition is thus situated, mediated, and distributed in the context:

> the cognitive properties of a group are not produced only by the internal structure of individuals, nor by the structure external to them. The cognitive properties of a group are produced by the interaction between the internal and external structures of individuals. (Hutchins, 1995, p. 262)

Therefore, with the expression "cognition in the wild," the author emphasized how knowledge is not a private suitcase of individuals but something that emerges and is distributed in the shared activity with others. This process of acquiring and distributing knowledge was described previously by Hutchins (1993) using a research study related to aspiring officers of the Canadian navy learning navigation techniques. Young officers were required to perform tasks assigned by senior officers, gradually exercising activities to increase decision-making autonomy. Interaction with more experienced colleagues allows navigators to learn the use of symbolic artifacts (such as maps and language) and materials (such as the complex technological instrumentation on ships): navigating is understood as an evolutionary, adaptive, cultural, and emergent process.

Hutchins (1995) highlighted how the redundancy of knowledge and the partial overlap within the group constitute essential prerequisites in the community of practice, allowing everyone to perform a single task competently.

Further, the understanding of each task by a member is strictly interconnected with the knowledge of the same practice by the other members, allowing optimal execution of the task. This process becomes a particular experience accessible to the entire community, essential for moving competently within the context. The functioning of the community is made possible by a significant relationship between individuals, tasks, and tools. To develop a shared image of what is happening, all participants must access relevant information (including free listening to conversations in which they are not directly involved). Equally important is the sharing of tacit or related knowledge. Technology's central role is delegated in these sharing processes, supporting intersubjectively shared understanding.

*Interpretative communities* (Feldman, 2002) emphasize the importance of interpretative repertoires to evaluate events, attribute meanings, understand reality, and create and modify specific interaction and action practices supported by the interpretative process. According to this perspective, participants create intersubjectivity by constructing new meanings. The generation of new meanings brings about discussion and participation, and interpretation generates, in turn, other meanings.

## Fluidity

In the actor-network theory (ANT), actors are individual entities (people, technologies, animals, texts, money, buildings, etc.) who take actions through which they can "exert detectable influence on others" (Law, 1987, p. 132). The underlying perspective is that a symmetric position exists in which humans are not given any priority over nonhumans in their ability to act.

Some typologies of actors have been identified in the emergence phase of an actor network:

- actors who are not identified by the network's objectives but are enrolled once agreement on the purposes proposed by the controlling actor is achieved;
- actors who might resist the roles they are supposed to play;
- actors who are disruptive and thus act against the network's interests; and
- actors who exercise control on behalf of the controlling actor.

Those not involved in the control process are not in that specific network.

An actor cannot exercise control alone, as Law highlights when discussing how the transformation of networks is achieved. She seeks to control others at a distance (1986, p. 255). Texts of all sorts, machines or other physical objects, and people, sometimes separately but more frequently in combination, seem to be the primary raw materials for the actor.

The actor introduces the "raw materials" that can introduce a degree of resistance and struggle (Law, 1992) at different moments during the translation process.

Belonging, participation, and fluidity are modalities of acting inside a collective. We can consider the three different approaches by the degree of connection, from more intense and continuous to lighter and more rarefied.

## A Concept, Technology, and a Metaphor

### Identity-Based Learning, Avatar & Cyborg, Virus

Learning is a social process, and entering a new community implies new learning. Simultaneously, learning is closely linked to, and arguably inseparable from, identity (Brown & Campione, 1990; Lave & Wenger, 1991). Learners begin to construct a professional identity within educational contexts because educational institutions cannot help but promote ways of being.

Cultivating a sense of who we are—and are becoming—is a continuous process of interpretation that does not have a stable character but is complex and shaped by personal and contextual factors. In the transaction from university to professional life, the question of who students can become is strongly influenced by the communities and institutions of which students are members (Cheneval-Armand & Impedovo, 2016). Being a professional involves more than understanding concepts and developing skills; it involves personal transformation as students become teachers, doctors, lawyers, psychologists, and so forth.

Today teachers are called to make many transitions during their professional life: from the school/faculty of education to the classroom, projects, involvement as researcher-practitioners, extended responsibilities as mentors and tutors, and more. At the same time, teachers are called to be responsive and accountable for urgent questions such as sustainability, violence, equity, and diversity adaptations.

The link between identity and learning brings more responsive action in the community and local context in which the action is undertaken: this brings out the process of *knowing in practice* (Gherardi, 2001); stresses the passage from the noun to the verb, suggesting that knowledge is an enactment and an accomplishment rather than a thing or a static property. As discussed by Gherardi, the possible focus is:

- *A pragmatic stance*. Practical knowledge is directed toward doing, making decisions in situations, solving problems, maintaining and reproducing a texture of practices.
- *A specific temporality*. Practical knowledge emerges from the situation and situated activities.
- *An anchoring in materiality*. Practical knowledge uses fragments of knowledge embedded in knowledgeable bodies, objects, technology, and the material world that interact with humans and interrogates them.
- *An anchoring in discursive practices*. Practical knowledge uses the discursive mobilization of cues for action and their positions within a narrative scheme that gives sense to what occurs in communication.
- *A historical-cultural anchoring*. Practical knowledge is also anchored by what has happened in the past and learned from experience and inexperience. If we consider the setting in which practices are accomplished, we must include its institutional context.

Postmodernism perspectives invite teachers to take ownership of the different forms of reading and interpreting reality, questioning Western philosophical and scientific tradition (Hayles, 2000, 2010). Postmodernism feeds new reflections on the professional dimension, becoming an open space for debate. Including other terminology such as, for example, post-humanism (meaning "after humanism" or "beyond humanism") opens the discourse to a new definition of humanity (Ferrando, 2019).

Post-humanism explores new cognition, perception, and developmental awareness implications (Belhassein et al., 2019) in a living era that deals with the Anthropocene, artificial intelligence, robots and robotics, ethical technology, genetic privacy, addiction to technology, environmental sustainability, power, equity, and so on.

The post-humanist perspectives invite us to consider the integrity of multispecies coexistence as comprehensive of the inorganic, including machines. Are we still human? Are we cyborgs? The term "cyborg" is applied to an organism with restored functions or enhanced abilities due to integrating some artificial component or technology that relies on feedback. Transhumanism challenges the current understanding of the human through the possibilities inscribed within its conceivable biological and technological evolutions. Machinic dignity is recognized together with human dignity, nonhuman-animal dignity, and bio-dignity.

Entities are searching to be part of and take advantage of a complex environment. The image selected here to discuss the entire process is the virus. In her keynote address for the Posthuman Mimesis conference, part of the ERC-funded HOM project, Katherine Hayles spoke about microbial resistance to viruses as a mimetic strategy for survival (https://www.youtube.com/watch?v=DP-OnWEjGus). For this, she relied on her double training in biology and literary theory to promote a mimetic turn in post-human studies. With roots in classical Greek drama and literary theory, mimesis is often regarded as primarily a discursive technique. However, Hayles recently argued that its embodied practice applications had expanded exponentially in an unexpected domain: microbial resistance to viruses.

The virus is, par excellence, the symbol of the entry into a new ecological system to transform it and let its impacts spread around, as the recent experiences of COVID-19 have shown. The virus metaphor shows how the preexisting community is a lived entity open to others, and the boundary signs the crossing line of transformation.

## For Learning Design

*E-belonging*

Belonging, participation, and fluidity can develop through different strategies and technologies. For the learning design of a teacher community, using online and digital tools is expected, giving space and modality to visualize processes and dynamics in socialization.

Online learning is already widely recognized as linked to self-learning and autonomy regulation, if we consider isolation and lack of social contact as inherent in this modality. Zoom and other video-conference systems have created a new form of recognized stress (Toney et al., 2021). Intimidating feelings have been reported by studies on online environments, such as the idea of posting to an online discussion forum site being felt as threatening (Whittaker & Kowalski, 2015).

Online or hybrid learning contexts affect a learner's sense of belonging through "the structure of the module, the behaviors of the tutors and the material, as well as the behavioral consequences of the learners" (Peacock et al., 2020, p. 26). The tutor's facilitation role is crucial in helping learners deepen their understanding in meaningful ways and increase a sense of belonging to support learner development. Resources that may be helpful to learners should be carefully mapped with clear signposting to prevent students from getting lost, feeling confused, alienated, or overwhelmed by the availability of an excessive supply of information. Careful program design with open and meaningful communication channels is essential, as is informed feedback from tutors who show genuine interest and concern, offer constructive feedback, and will once again strengthen the bond between learner and tutor. Such commitments can reinforce a sense of belonging. In table 2.1, we propose a script for an online short course that will assist in developing a sense of participation.

Table 2.1. Example of Script for a Collaborative Short Course

| Activity | Description | Time | Modality | Temporality | Proposed Tools | Facilitator's Role |
|---|---|---|---|---|---|---|
| Pre-session activity | Please think of one definition for "collaborative learning" and its features. Confront your colleagues and read together with resources and references. | 15 min. | Individual | Asynchronous | Padlet Forum | Invitation and welcome |
| Group work | Suggestions on how to hybridize a training course for adult education | 15 min. | Collective | Synchronous | Wiki | Introduction; the concept of scripts and features for adult education |
| Group work | Sharing experiences about a course | 10 min. | Collective | Synchronous | Zoom Wiki | Split into groups |
| Group work | Applying the rules: how to conceive your ideal hybrid course | 5 min. | Collective | Synchronous | Padlet | Assign resources to each group |
| BREAK | Cooking recipe challenge | 5 min. | Collective | Synchronous | Gather. town app | Supervise the challenge |
| Brainstorming | Guideline to rethink your course based on the ideal hybrid course; justification of features | 20 min. | Collective | Asynchronous | Wiki | Check productions and give feedback |
| Feedback | Assessment, meta-reflection, and sharing scripts | 10 min. | Individual | Asynchronous | Wiki | Give follow-up perspectives |

## TAKEAWAY IDEAS FROM THIS CHAPTER

### Reflecting on the Sense of Belonging and Identity

In this chapter, we delved into the sense of belonging that we experience as a member of a professional community. Obviously, this issue needs to be considered in relation to the process of becoming a professional in that professional community. Many theoretical frameworks are discussed in the section above, and you must have read them by considering your professional identity and the sense of belonging to your community that you have established over the years.

Here, let's think again about what you have gone through and construct your takeaways from this chapter. First, reflect on the sense of belonging you have in your workplace as you recall interactions with your colleagues and consider your role in the professional community. Your sense of belonging in your professional community could have been originated in the ways you have interacted with others in your workplace. Your memories of these experiences might not have been very clear, but wear a new lens (i.e., new theoretical frameworks discussed above) and see how you could look at your experiences more clearly—and possibly differently.

As in the previous chapter, the following questions will guide you in this journey. Try to use the referenced theoretical frameworks to answer them as much as possible, as you did in the previous chapter. Be aware that facts do not change over time, but memories do not stay unchanged. As you engage in critical reflections on your experiences, you may be able to deconstruct your experiences in your professional community and develop a new understanding.

- Looking back to the past few weeks, what social interactions stand out? With whom and what were they about? How do you think these social interactions could characterize your role and identity in the professional community?
- To what extent do you think your professional identity reflects your relationship to your professional community? How has your relationship to your professional community changed over the years due to interactions and experiences with your colleagues?
- You must have made many decisions that shaped who you are as a professional. For example, you could have established your identity as a collaborative colleague and focused on improving teaching with your colleagues—or you could have focused on independently improving your teaching. You must have made many such choices, which could define who you are in the community. How would you reflect on your decision making and choices that shaped your professional identity? Consider what you

value and cherish as a professional as well as how you could further grow and develop as a member of your professional community.
- What objectives or visions of your professional community influence the ways you interact with your colleagues and define your professional identity in your workplace? In what ways do you think the objectives and visions of your professional community influence your sense of belonging to the professional community? How do you feel about it? Is there any underlying value system?
- In early years, you might have focused on surviving and juggling all kinds of tasks in your workplace, but then you gradually must have achieved professional competence to complete all kinds of tasks without much effort. As you work with your colleagues, you might have learned to contribute to your professional community as an experienced teacher recognized by others. In this process, you might have created close ties with your colleagues and focused more on creating a school policy that shapes the nature of your teacher community. What do you think causes such a shift? To what extent do you think you have contributed to the development of your teacher community?
- Do you feel that a gap exists between the role that you would like to play and the role you do play in your professional community? What seems to be creating such a gap, and how do you think you can narrow that gap?
- In your professional life, you could have gone out of your department and come to know people outside it—or you could have focused on interacting only with people in your department. Do you see people other than your immediate colleagues and outside of your professional community from whom you can learn new things that contribute to your professional life? If so, what did you learn from such experiences? If not, what is preventing you from doing it? How rigid or open do you feel social networks and communities are in your workplace?
- When and how did technology and online space come to play a role in defining your professional identity? To what extent is your professional identity rooted in the technology or online spaces you use? In your workplace, what skills and understanding of technology and online space do you think are essential to qualify you as a member of the professional community?
- Do you feel that online and hybrid interactions empower you? What potential risks do you see? What kinds of dialogues do you think should be taking place in online and physical space, and how are online and physical social space influencing each other at your workplace?
- How do you envision the future role of online and hybrid interactions in your workplace? How do you think they influence the sense of belonging of the members of your professional community? What should be actualized in the future?

# REFERENCES

Allen, K. A., & Bowles, T. (2012). Belonging as a guiding principle in the education of adolescents. *Australian Journal of Educational & Developmental Psychology,* 12, 108–119.

Anderman, L. H., & Freeman, T. M. (2004). Students' sense of belonging in school. In P. R. Pintrich & M. L. Maehr (Eds.), *Advances in motivation and achievement: Motivating students, improving schools: The legacy of Carol Midgley* (vol. 13, pp. 27–63). JAI Press. http://dx.doi.org/10.1016/S0749-7423(03)13002-6

Belhassein, K., Cochet, H., Clodic, A., Guidetti, M., & Alami, R. (2019, July). From children to robots: How the parallel with developmental psychology can improve human-robot joint activities. Joint Action Meeting (JAM), Gênes, Italy.

Brown, A. L., & Campione, J. C. (1990). Interactive learning environments and the teaching of science and mathematics. In M. Gardner (Ed.), *Toward a scientific practice of science education* (pp. 111–139). L. Erlbaum Associates.

Cheneval-Armand, H., & Impedovo, M. A. (2016). Learning trajectories and professional development: Student-teacher in electrical engineering. *Review of Science, Mathematics and ICT Education, 10*(1), 93–114.

Feldman, C. (2002). The construction of mind and self in an interpretative community. In J. Brockmeier, M. Wang, & D. R. Olson (Eds.), *Literacy, narrative and culture* (pp. 52–66). Curzon.

Ferrando, F. (2019). *Philosophical posthumanism*. Bloomsbury Publishing.

Gaskins, W. B., Johnson, J., Maltbie, C., & Kukreti, A. (2015). Changing the learning environment in the college of engineering and applied science using challenge-based learning. *International Journal of Engineering Pedagogy, 5*(1), 33. https://doi.org/10.3991/ijep.v5i1.4138

Gherardi, S. (2001). From organizational learning to practice-based knowing. *Human Relations, 54*(1), 131–139.

Gherardi, S. (2019). *Practice as a collective and knowledgeable doing*. Universität Siegen: SFB 1187 Medien der Kooperation 2019 (SFB 1187 Medien der Kooperation—Working Paper Series 8). https://doi.org/10.25969/mediarep/12641

Goodenow, C. (1993). Classroom belonging among early adolescent students: Relationships to motivation and achievement. *Journal of Early Adolescence, 13*(1), 21–43. https://doi.org/10.1177/0272431693013001002

Goodwin, C. (1994). Professional vision. *American Anthropologist, 96*(3), 600–633.

Hayles, N. K. (2000). *How we became posthuman: Virtual bodies in cybernetics, literature, and informatics*. University of Chicago Press.

Hayles, N. K. (2010). How we became posthuman: Ten years on an interview with N. Katherine Hayles. *Paragraph*, 318–330.

Hutchins, E. (1993). Learning to navigate. In S. Chaiklin & J. Lave (Eds.), *Understanding practice: Perspectives on activity and context* (pp. 35–63). Cambridge University Press.

Hutchins, E. (1995). *Cognition in the wild*. MIT Press.

Janosz, M., Georges, P., & Parent, S. (1998). L'environnement socioéducatif à l'école secondaire: Un modèle théorique pour guider l'évaluation du milieu. *Revue canadienne de psycho-éducation, 27*(2), 285–306.

Lave, J., & Wenger, E. (1991). *Situated learning: Legitimate peripheral participation*. Cambridge University Press.

Law, J. (1986). On power and its tactics: A view from the sociology of science. *The Sociological Review, 34*(1), 1–38.

Law, J. (1987). The structure of sociotechnical engineering: A review of the new sociology of technology. *The Sociological Review, 35*(2), 405–425.

Law, J. (1992). Notes on the actor-network theory: Ordering, strategy, and heterogeneity. *Systems Practice, 5*(4), 379–393.

Lewin, K. (1951). *Field theory in social science; Selected theoretical papers*. D. Cartwright (Ed.). Harper & Row.

Moreland, R. L., & Levine, J. M. (1989). Newcomers and old-timers in small groups. In P. B. Paulus (Ed.), *Psychology of time* (pp. 143–186). Erlbaum.

Moreland, R. L., & Levine, J. M. (2014). Socialization in organizations and work groups. In *Groups at Work* (pp. 83–126). Psychology Press.

Orr, J. E. (1990). Sharing knowledge, celebrating identity: Community memory in a service culture. In D. Middleton & D. Edwards (Eds.), *Collective remembering* (pp. 169–189). SAGE.

Osterman, K. F. (2010). Teacher practice and students' sense of belonging. In T. Lovat, R. Toomey, & R. Clement (Eds.), *International research handbook on values education and student wellbeing* (pp. 239–260). Springer.

Peacock, S., & Cowan, J. (2019). Promoting a sense of belonging in online learning communities of inquiry in accredited courses. *Online Learning, 23*(2), 67–81.

Peacock, S., Cowan, J., Irvine, L., & Williams, J. (2020). An exploration into the importance of a sense of belonging for online learners. *International Review of Research in Open and Distributed Learning, 21*(2), 18–35.

Toney, S., Light, J., & Urbaczewski, A. (2021). Fighting Zoom fatigue: Keeping the zoombies at bay. *Communications of the Association for Information Systems, 48*(1), 10.

van Gennep, A. (1909). *Les rites de passage*. Paris.

Wenger, E. (1998). *Communities of practice, learning, meaning, and identity*. Cambridge University Press.

Wenger, E. (2000). Communities of practice and social learning systems. *Organization, 7*(2), 225–246.

Whittaker, E., & Kowalski, R. M. (2015). Cyberbullying via social media. *Journal of School Violence, 14*(1), 11–29.

Wood, D., Bruner, J. S., & Ross, G. (1976). The role of tutoring in problem-solving. *Journal of Child Psychology and Psychiatry, 17*, 89–100.

Zazzo, B. (1984). *L'école maternelle à deux ans: Oui ou non?* Stock-Laurence Perdoud.

*Chapter Three*

# Socialization into a Teacher Collective

"Kitty, dear, let's pretend—" And here I wish I could tell you half the things Alice used to say, beginning with her favourite phrase, "Let's pretend." She had had quite a long argument with her sister only the day before— all because Alice had begun with "Let's pretend we're kings and queens;" and her sister, who liked being very exact, had argued that they couldn't, because there were only two of them, and Alice had been reduced at last to say, "Well, you can be one of them then, and I'll be all the rest."
—L. Carroll (2010)

Thinking about the level of organization, structure, and connections to the structure is the first step to creating a collective of teachers—focusing on approach and correspondent technological solutions. The entry into the community must be proposed to individual teachers as an identity and emotional experience, with new possibilities along the way. Living inside a community means socializing at different levels. As Carroll's quote shows, the challenge is to find the collective dimensions expressed in the action and the perspective of individual participation, a true expression of collective learning and knowledge building.

## THREE PERSPECTIVES

After teachers join the group, the goal is to let them remain in the group of their interest, starting a socialization process that makes them influential members. According to Brim's (1966) classic definition, socialization is "the process by which individuals acquire the knowledge, skills, feelings, and behaviors that enable them to participate, as more or less efficient members, in social life" (p. 3). By socialization, we mean an interactive process through which individuals acquire the knowledge, skills, and dispositions that allow them to participate meaningfully in the reality surrounding them.

When an individual enters a new environment, she must meet the group's demands regarding how they relate to the other people she interacts with and simultaneously try to meet her own needs. The relationship between the newcomer and the insertion context is not always straightforward. This section explores three perspectives: *behavior* in a traditional social psychology approach, *practice*, and *connections*.

## Behavior

In the 1970s and 1980s, different models of socialization were developed, classified as follows by Ashforth, Sluss, and Harrison (2007):

- The first set of models distinguished socialization as fixed and linear sequences.
- The second set of models, defined as "integrative models" (Wanous, 1977), recognized the weakness of the previous models and tended to attribute a more conceptual rather than predictive value to these phased models because they could provide valuable heuristics to conceptualize the changes that newcomers and organizations face in the socialization process.
- A final set of models are defined as "specialized models." They acknowledge a more fluid nature at the various stages given by the specificity of each socialization path, influenced by different contextual and distinctive elements.

According to Moreland and Levine (1989), group membership can be described as a series of five phases separated by respective role transitions:

1. As seen in the previous chapter, the first phase is *exploration*, which, once satisfied, allows the new member to enter the group effectively.
2. In the second phase of *socialization*, the group ensures that the individual's behavior is helpful to the group's life. At the same time, the newcomer will try to bring about changes to satisfy his personal needs: if these two situations come into contact, then full acceptance exists, and the newcomer becomes a group member.
3. The third phase is *maintenance*, which is necessary to maintain the balance between all the components: if this does not happen, divergences or conflicts may arise. This divergence within the group that oversees the individual could lead to the member being marginalized from the group.

4. The fourth phase is *resocialization*. The individual and the group try to improve the situation by clarifying the role of each in the group, making convergence possible. If this convergence does not occur, the individual leaves the group.
5. The final phase is *remembrance*, in which the individual is considered an ex-member, and what binds him to the group is only a mutual memory.

This type of socialization was initially considered a process of social influence with the transmission of information, values, and behavioral models that the subject must employ to succeed in the workplace. Subsequently, a theoretical perspective was developed that appears more suitable for enhancing the critical position of the subject who "socializes": we try to understand how the subject appropriates social reality and how he maintains an active role in the process of influence in which he is involved.

Socialization appears, therefore, as a negotiation process in which the subject and the group interact mutually, influencing each other circularly and continuously. The group can employ "socialization tactics" as first classified by Van Maanen and Schein (1979) and attributable to two fundamental strategies:

1. An *institutional* strategy: formal, collective, and preestablished socialization activities that offer the newcomer a highly formalized way of interpreting her role and exercising the task; and
2. An *individual* strategy: ways of socializing with informal integration practices leave the newcomer ample room to develop a personal approach to the task and role. This process occurs mainly through interactions and exchanges with other organization members, direct observation, and the search for feedback.

Studies show that direct tactics are used mainly to obtain technical information, whereas indirect techniques tend to be used for organizational and social information. The newcomer has an active role in determining his insertion in a work group, implementing "proactive" behavior (Morrison, 1993), understood as the information-seeking effort to influence the course of socialization.

Chao et al. (1994) recognized the fundamental role of supervisory relationships, especially informal ones, which characterize the social learning process of the newcomer: thanks to this, the newcomer not only perfects technical skills but recognizes and acquires the essential elements of the productive and organizational structure.

Social psychology has been concerned with social influence processes from the very beginning. By social influence, we mean a change in an individual's judgments, opinions, and attitudes due to exposure to other individuals' decisions, opinions, and attitudes. This can occur in any situation. There are two *social entities*: one is the source of influence and the other is the target. These two interact through an "object," which can be an opinion or a behavior.

The most famous experiment in this research field is Asch's (1952). Asch concluded that the drive to make one's judgment conform to that of others is not unconscious but is based on a completely conscious reasoning process of evaluation. The type of conformism that emerges is informative social influence: when the individual finds herself in ambiguous situations, she assumes the behavior of others and adapts unconsciously.

So, people are influenced by each other as a source of information to produce an answer together. Milgram (1974) explained this result with the concept of a *heteronomous state*: a person inserted in an authoritarian system passes from an autonomous state to a state in which she no longer feels free to act because she has to satisfy the needs of others.

Earlier, Moscovici (1972) focused his attention on the influence exercised by individuals or minority groups: the purpose of any majority social entity is to exercise social control; the purpose of minority social entities is innovation, changing majority positions. Festinger (1957) considered that uniformity increases in new or ambiguous situations because fewer "objective" elements guide our judgments. Without uniformity in the group, achieving the goal would not be easy. He made the distinction between

- the informative influence as the force that pushes an isolated individual to accept information as evidence about reality, and
- the normative influence as the force that pushes an individual, as a group member, to respond in a manner consistent with the positive expectations of one or more group members.

The pressure leads to public compliance but not absolute conformity: socially acceptable responses are replicated in public, and beliefs are maintained in private.

In addition, Festinger (1957) spoke of information referents: belonging to a group provides social identity as individuals associate themselves with the attributes and norms they perceive as part of the group.

A specific phenomenon of importance to teacher communities is group polarization, first studied by Stoner (1961): group decisions are more risk-oriented than individual choices. Subsequent research has shown that, in reality, the shift did not go toward risk but toward the direction that initially prevailed. In fact, according to existing normative processes, members try to conform to the group norm, which is accepted by the majority, and enhance their image by taking the most extreme position in the favored direction.

Moscovici and Doise (1991) identified normalized decisions (which move closer to the average) and most innovative choices (which move away from the individual average). In "groupthink," the desire to reach a consensus interferes with everyday decision-making skills, with too much importance given to consent over dissent.

## Practice

According to Wenger (1991), learning is pervasive in every life situation and intensifies in circumstances when new situations occur and challenges are to be solved. Knowledge is explicit (manifest) and tacit (understood as implicit knowledge linked to personal experience). This distinction recalls the distinction between "know-how" (knowing how) and "know that" (knowing that), where "knowledge runs along the tracks of practice" (Brown & Duguid, 2001) and makes the circulation of knowledge possible.

Learning, according to Wenger (1998), is strictly connected to two concepts, participation and reification:

1. *Participation* refers to the social experience of living in the world through belonging to social communities, including forms such as collaboration or even conflict-type relationships. Recognizing themselves as active participants in the same community leads members to share experiences of meaning. The group plays a central role in favoring or hindering the access of participants and newcomers to information relevant to the proper functioning of a distributed cognition system (Hutchins, 1995).
2. *Reification* transforms practices and experiences into symbols, stories, artifacts, and concepts. They persist over time but are constantly exposed to new and multiple interpretations and reinterpretation processes.

The two concepts should be understood as "a single conceptual unit," the two processes being sources of discontinuity (changing and assuming new positions) and continuity (through memories and stories). Participation represents an interpretative criterion to correct the potential limits of reification (such as immobility and rigidity); reification stabilizes involvement that could be excessively confusing and ambiguous. Participation and reification can be causes of discontinuity, as happens when a new member enters the group or new technology is introduced, which forces the whole group to new balances and changes.

The social structure that this process creates is emergent and open because the practice derives from the negotiation process between the members, capable of including new elements and restructuring existing meanings. In practice, learning is also seen in investment (Wenger, 1998), which involves the individual's identity and derives from reciprocal relationships, a well-defined company, and a well-organized repertoire.

Therefore, learning does not require abstract notions and concepts but complete absorption made possible by effective participation in the community of practice (Lave & Wenger, 1991).

Participation in the community of practice is based on discursive strategies manifested in conversations, formal meetings, or informal chats during lunch breaks. Rogoff (1995) uses the expression "appropriation" to indicate the change due to the newcomer's participation in the activity. Learning can, therefore, be described as an apprenticeship process, a metaphor Rogoff uses to understand contextualized practice, inserted in a context achieved through guided participation by the other members in the processes and communication systems to involve and carry out culturally relevant activities for the group.

The concept of guided participation is an interpersonal relationship. It can be implicit or explicit, carried out by familiar people or strangers, organized through systematic instructions or accidental comments made during activity performance. Conversation results from a complex intertwining of activities by two or more individuals who interact and progressively build the meaning of their actions based on shared cultural backgrounds, and a common and general willingness to communicate.

The "guidance" referred to in guided participation involves the direction offered by cultural and social values, as well as social partners; the "participation" in guided participation relates to observation, as well as hands-on involvement in an activity (Rogoff, 1995). The result is a "participatory appropriation" in which competence is achieved through carrying out an activity and becoming prepared for related activities: one does not learn information "about the practices" but "becomes" a practitioner (Brown & Duguid, 2001, p. 341); thus, it involves a process of becoming and not one of acquisition.

A conversation becomes the privileged place to implement an explicit negotiation and redefinition of shared values, learning to become a recognized member of one's community of practice. The sequence of collective discursive acts and the intentionality of the participants in the interaction give meaning to sharing.

The collective construction of meaning is a necessary condition for learning. The center of the analysis becomes the social and discursive construction of reality, understood as the product of those continuous negotiations between individuals that allow reaching an intersubjective consensus on the meanings of actions. Socialization, therefore, becomes a constant learning process, implying forms of continuity and discontinuity.

## Connection

In a network, stability occurs through some form of control.

Law (1986) talks about "inscriptions" as controlling actors without being influenced by others. The more an inscription can maintain its relational patterns for longer, the more durable it is. The more an inscription can link the core (e.g., the controlling actor) and the periphery (e.g., other actors), the more opportunities for an inscription to become mobile. So, there is the production of a prescribed way to act toward others.

Behavior, practices, and connections are the links to achieving efficient management of a teacher community.

## One Concept, One Technology, and One Metaphor

*Participatory Sense Making, Robotics, and Boundary*

Fuchs and De Jaegher (2009) explain the concept of participatory sense making as an interactive process involving all the participants in the contest:

> Meanings and intentions may be formed not only individually but arise through participatory sense-making. They are emergent products of interaction, and in many situations, they can be viewed as distributed phenomena rather than as individual, private mental acts or properties. (p. 480)

Meaning is cocreated in a way not necessarily attributable to either of the interaction partners, but it is participative. The other already affects who each is within the interaction. The "in-between" becomes the source of the operative intentionality of both partners. This partner is not only human. Technology is reshaping the micro-ecologies of developing, becoming a part of it. It impacts and enables reconfiguration of social interaction in everyday situations.

The technology that could be considered in this process of socializing is the robot. In particular, social robotics is a fast-growing research field geared toward the design and study of "autonomous" robots expected to engage in social interaction with humans. Considering that social robots have a physical body, new possible social and material reconfiguration interactions emerge into the robots' interactions, as shown by the work of Hasse (2020). More, several studies show the implications of introducing social and anthropological robots inside the "indigenous classroom," where baby humans are already present (see the works of Alač, 2016; Solberg, 2021). The robot's presence in the classroom will increase shortly. Sharkey (2016) proposes four scenarios: the robot as a classroom teacher, the robot embedding teacher telepresence, the robot as companion and peer, and the robot as a care-eliciting companion.

The physical or virtual boundary in natural and present spaces clarifies a group's existence. Boundaries are generally understood as something that borders two or more entities. They can be semiotic (such as a road sign) and material (such as the yellow line indicating the area for compliance of privacy), but also intangible and invisible (such as the distance between people in an elevator). Therefore, the concept of the border involves a multidisciplinary perspective, which involves psychology and linguistics. In business, we keep dividing everything into parts and distinguishing objects from each other; we attribute some sense to the individual parts of a whole, bringing out new dynamics that regulate our relationship with the whole: "There is a multiplicity of practices, inclusive and exclusive, and, based to the context, a multiplicity of ways in which things are delimited" (Beck, 2003, p. 24). The borders create signs and are temporary structures for hierarchical organization of acting, behavior, feeling, and thinking.

## For Learning Design

### Role Taking

In line with the main socio-constructivist theories, students' interaction needs to be promoted and structured according to specific scaffolds, mainly applied to digital environments. Effective and significant collaborative learning requires structured interactions drawn around scripts and roles assigned to students.

Many learning strategies have proven to help promote active and constructive participation. Among them, we focus on role taking. Role taking is a helpful scaffolding tool for effective collaborative learning because it is based on the provision of collaborative scripts; these scripts—or task assignments—seem to help students: they should be well defined and anchored to precise pedagogical models. Literature (Suh, 2011) shows how role taking effectively supports collaborative knowledge building and socio-relational processes between group members, especially when combined with other strategies, such as specific attention to the characteristics of the assigned task, an appropriate configuration of the digital environment, and an adequate composition of the groups.

Moreover, supporting social interaction through role taking seems to assist in acquiring individual and social agency, enabling every group member to participate and grow.

## TAKEAWAY IDEAS FROM THIS CHAPTER

### Reflecting on Socialization Processes

In this chapter, we discussed how various factors define the process of socialization in a professional community. Social dynamics in an organization can be quite complex and largely invisible, so the process of socialization is not an easy thing to reflect on. But socialization takes place every day in your workplace, and it can be a defining factor for the development of a teacher community.

Especially for newcomers, this process must make quite a strong and lasting impression of the professional community. You may remember how you got socialized to your current colleagues in your first year and how you settled down in your workplace. In the process, you might have felt a certain level of connection (or frustration) to some colleagues whereas you might have wondered why you could not feel the same way when it came to others. This might have created a quite strong tone for you to become a part of your professional community. And this is not limited to you. This applies to almost everyone in any professional community.

To reflect further, consider the teacher committee you belong to. Remember when the new committee was formed and the first meeting was scheduled at the beginning of the school year. Before the meeting, you might have checked who were on the committee and felt relaxed if the colleagues you felt close to were on the committee. In the first meeting, you could have felt at ease in speaking up and sharing your ideas frankly if your close colleague(s) sat at the same table. Similarly, the nature of social interactions, problem solving, and decision making in a workplace could depend on the ways community members have been socialized with each other. In the process, there must be a number of psychological, political, and cultural factors that dynamically interact and influence the nature of interactions. The process can be quite organic and complex to decipher, but it is an important issue in considering a teacher professional community.

Reflecting on the nature of the socialization process in your workplace is essential if we want to truly support new community members' professional development. In your workplace, perhaps newcomers are socialized in a sink-or-swim fashion. Or they could be approached by experienced members of your community and offered informal or formal introductions to other community members with a carefully configured support system from the very beginning. The mentorship offered to newcomers could be stipulated in a manual, but the support system could also be shared implicitly by experienced community members.

This is an essential issue to consider because if newcomers are left on their own and fail to socialize with other community members, they may be unable to develop a sense of belonging to the community. Similarly, without carefully reflecting on the socialization processes, the extent to which people co-construct new knowledge, skills, and wisdom would be highly limited. Reflect on this issue and construct your own takeaways from this chapter. As you did in earlier chapters, consider the following issues as you think about the theoretical and conceptual frameworks just discussed:

- Think about a series of meetings that you attended recently at your workplace. How did you participate in these meetings? How do you choose to comment on some ideas while choosing not to comment on others? To what extent is your choice related to your social relationship to the members present at the meetings?
- When you were new, how were you introduced and welcomed to the school community? How did you get socialized to other members of the school community, and what kind of socialization did you anticipate happening back then? How did you feel about the process? How do you see your relationship to the school community change over time and why? What could be improved?
- What do you think about the ways newcomers are introduced and socialized at your workplace now? What kind of mentorship or support is given to them? From whom do they learn about social structure and social dynamics in your workplace? Do mentors get assigned to them, and do newcomers receive mentorship in your workplace? If not, why?
- Using the teacher committee that you belong to as an example, draw a network diagram that includes key players, key forces, and factors that seem to define the social dynamics there. Do you see any possibility of improvement based on the network diagram? Is it possible to incorporate a new system for the members so that they can get socialized better with each other and co-construct new knowledge and skills with others?
- In a recent teacher meeting you participated in, how were issues discussed? Do you think that the participants in the meetings were able to co-construct new knowledge and skills in the social interactions taking place? Did they make good decisions? If not, why? What needs to be improved?
- How do you see the social dynamics in your professional community change over the years? What direction are these dynamics taking, and why? What kinds of change are needed?
- What roles do technology, including online space and social network systems, play in the socialization process? What analytical lens is useful to make sense of these roles in your professional community? And what

would you like to see happening in terms of the use of technology and online space?
- How have robots and artificial intelligence (AI) been introduced and used for work in your workplace? What do you think of their roles and potential in your professional community? How do these nonhuman agents change the ways socialization takes place in your workplace?
- What potentials and risks do you see regarding the socialization of the members of your professional community in the post-COVID era? Today, how are members of your professional community embracing new technology and online space for socialization? What difference does this make in terms of the ways people get socialized and communicate in your workplace? What actions do you think are necessary to improve people's relationship to technology and online space in your workplace now?

## REFERENCES

Alač, Morana. (2016). Social robots: Things or agents? *AI & Society, 31*(4), 519–535.

Asch, S. E. (1952). *Social psychology*. Prentice-Hall.

Ashforth, B. E., Sluss, D. M., & Harrison, S. H. (2007). Socialization in organizational contexts. In G. P. Hodgkinson & J. K. Ford (Eds.), *International review of industrial and organizational psychology* (Vol. 22, pp. 1–70). Wiley.

Beck, U. (2003). *La société du risque: Sur la voie d'une autre modernité*. Flammarion–Champs.

Brim, O. (1966). Socialization through the life cycle. In O. Brim & H. Wheeler (Eds.), *Socialization after childhood: Two essays*. Wiley.

Brown, J. S., & Duguid, P. (2001). Communities of practice. *Organization Science, 12*(2).

Carroll, L. (2010). *Through the looking glass and what Alice found there*. Penguin UK.

Chao, G. T., O'Leary-Kelly, A. M., Wolf, S., Klein, H. J., & Gardner, P. D. (1994). Organizational socialization: Its content and consequences. *Journal of Applied Psychology, 79*(5), 730.

Festinger, L. (1957). *A theory of cognitive dissonance*. Stanford University Press.

Fuchs, T., & De Jaegher, H. (2009). Enactive intersubjectivity: Participatory sense-making and mutual incorporation. *Phenomenology and the Cognitive Sciences, 8*(4), 465–486.

Hasse, C. (2020). *Posthumanist learning: What robots and cyborgs teach us about being ultra-social*. Routledge.

Hutchins, E. (1995). *Cognition in the wild*. MIT Press.

Lave, J., & Wenger, E. (1991). *Situated learning: Legitimate peripheral participation*. Cambridge University Press.

Law, J. (1986). Editor's introduction: Power/Knowledge and the dissolution of the sociology of knowledge. In J. Law (Ed.), *Power, action and belief: A new sociology of knowledge?* Routledge & Kegan Paul.

Milgram, S. (1974). *Obedience to authority: An experimental view*. Harper & Row.

Moreland, R. L., & Levine, J. M. (1989). Newcomers and old-timers in small groups. In P. B. Paulus (Ed.), *Psychology of time* (pp. 143–186). Erlbaum.

Morrison, E. W. (1993). A longitudinal study of the effects of information seeking on newcomer socialization. *Journal of Applied Psychology, 78*, pp. 173–183.

Moscovici, S. (1972). Theory and society in social psychology. In J. Israel & H. Tajfel (Eds.), *The context of social psychology: A critical assessment*. Academic Press.

Moscovici, S., & Doise, W. (1991). *Dissensions et consensus. Une théorie générale des décisions collectives*. Presses Universitaires de France.

Rogoff, B. (1995). Observing sociocultural activity on three planes: Participatory appropriation, guided participation, and apprenticeship. In J. V. Wertsch, P. del Rio, & A. Alvarez (Eds.), *Sociocultural studies of mind* (pp. 139–164). Cambridge University Press.

Sharkey, A. J. (2016). Should we welcome robot teachers? *Ethics and Information Technology, 18*(4), 283–297.

Solberg, M. (2021). *A cognitive ethnography of knowledge and material culture: Cognition, experiment, and the science of salmon lice*. Springer Nature.

Stoner, J. A. F. (1961). *A comparison of individual and group decisions involving risk* (Doctoral dissertation). Massachusetts Institute of Technology.

Suh, H. (2011). Collaborative learning models and support technologies in the future classroom. *International Journal for Educational Media and Technology, 5*(1), 50–61.

Van Maanen, J., & Schein, E. H. (1979). Toward a theory of organizational socialization. *Research in Organizational Behavior, 1*, 209–264.

Wanous, J. P. (1977). Organizational entry: The individual's viewpoint. In J. R. Hackman, E. Lawler, & L. Porter (Eds.), *Perspectives on behavior in organizations* (pp. 126–135). McGraw-Hill.

Wenger, G. C. (1991). A network typology: From theory to practice. *Journal of Aging Studies, 5*(2), 147–162.

Wenger, E. (1998). *Communities of practice: Learning, meaning and identity*. Cambridge University Press.

*Chapter Four*

# Development of a Teacher Community

All of the processes we encounter have a life cycle and transform over time. Knowing theoretical models of the evolution of collective processes helps us think about the community that we want to put into action, to understand, direct, and strengthen.

## THREE PERSPECTIVES

In the following, we consider some perspectives of the development of a teacher community: growth, cycle, and translation.

### Growth

The primary model that proposes group development is that of McMurrain and Gazda (1974). Starting from the analysis of their conversations, the authors identified four stages in the development of a group:

1. *Exploratory*: group members are hesitant to interact and tackle everyday tasks, probably due to the need to get to know each other.
2. *Transition*: in this phase, the members agree on the methods of discussion; at the same time, they prepare the rules that structure the work context.
3. *Action*: attention is focused on the objective of the discussion, which brings together the attention of all participants.
4. *Conclusion*: as the closure of the business approaches and the achievement of the common goal, participants face the conflict generated between the positive feelings linked to having formed a functional group and the negative ones due to the imminent dissolution.

An earlier theorization was proposed by Tuckman (1965), who elaborated a model relating to the "becoming" of the group according to the natural development processes of the individual from birth to adult maturity. The model develops in five consecutive stages:

1. *Forming*: the initial phase during which the members are oriented mainly concerning the behavior to be followed and the nature of the objective to be achieved. This is a start-up period in which the components depend on the leader, subject to more or more minor explicit requests on what to do.
2. *Storming*: a phase in which members discuss and ask themselves what problem they need to solve, how they work independently and together, and define what kind of leadership they accept. This phase is necessary for the team's growth, even if it can be stressful for members who are not used to the conflict. The leadership style can soften the manifestation of these problems, making the crisis implicit and not functional to the quality of the task. After this stage, many groups fail to develop, not knowing how to manage the conflict.
3. *Norming*: the group is organized around a common goal, indicating a newfound positive climate, elaborating rules that regulate the relationship life between the participants and the carrying out of tasks, the free circulation of information, and mutual trust. All members assume responsibility and ambition toward the operation and success of the activities. The danger is the desire to avoid conflict and share controversial ideas.
4. *Performing*: the group is motivated and focuses on the task, positively resolving the relational problems. The group works productively and competently without external supervision, making decisions autonomously.
5. *Adjourning*: it concerns the final phase of the group, the one that precedes the dissolution, and is characterized by a certain disengagement, above all emotional. Regarding the last point of adjourning, Levine and Moreland (1994) distinguish between optimistic and pessimistic adjourning: in the first, members think that their group may dissolve in the future but are convinced that, through their joint effort, they delay or prevent this event from happening; the pessimistic adjourning is noted for a decline in activities, and the group becomes unable to carry out the usual tasks, giving way to negative feelings.

The model proposes the development of the group as an evolutionary process characterized by the importance of relational exchanges. The formation and development of the group are homogeneous, modifying individual conduct, processes of group formation, and relationships established with other groups.

Worchel et al.'s (1991) model is cyclical and consists of six phases:

1. *Period of discontent*: it is the starting condition for forming a new group based on a previously existing one that has already achieved goals but whose members no longer see a prospect of development for the future. The dominant feelings are disappointment, discontent, apathy, and motivation to undertake new activities.
2. *Precipitating event*: it is a breaking event (such as a public demonstration, the expulsion of some members from the group, the adoption by the group of a new statute, etc.) that becomes the spark for the formation of a new group, distancing themselves from the "core" members of the previous group. The precipitating events give members the hope of bringing about changes through joint action.
3. *Group identification*: the new group is engaged in constructing its own identity, defining an internal structure composed of generally centralized leadership, norms and values, and different roles. In this phase, the group tries to draw its boundaries and, therefore, does not willingly accept newcomers, compromising the functioning.
4. *Group productivity*: the group has defined its own strong identity. It assesses members based on their skills to better focus on achieving the goals. Leadership is also assigned based on the skill highlighted. The analysis of group resources ensures that attention is also directed to other groups to recover additional resources and skills necessary to achieve the objectives. Conflicts are avoidant so as not to divert attention from achieving the goal.
5. *Individuation*: in this phase of group life, the individual members evaluate their contribution to the group's life and begin to ask themselves how satisfactory the group is for them. The desire for social recognition and the idea that other groups could better appreciate individual contributions decrease individual effort in group productivity. New members are actively sought for new resources and alternative points of view. The heterogeneity in the group increases, and they explore the possibility of withdrawing from the group.
6. *Decline*: in this last phase of the group, discontent becomes shared and reciprocal, definitively compromising the ability to carry out activities and achieve objectives. The group's/groups' identity is questioned, criticism of leadership increases, and scapegoats are sought to attribute failures. As a result, they spread under groups, and social inertia among the members demotivates and paralyzes the group. The conditions are created to spread discontent, eventually leading to some members founding a new group.

## Cycle

Wenger (2000) identified five possible stages in the development of communities of practice, not necessarily consequential:

1. *Potential*: in this phase, the members carry out activities such as research and discovery of others and the community. Given the start-up phase, people share similar work situations without enjoying the real benefit of sharing practices.
2. *Coalescing*: members activate the exploration of possible connections, the definition of a joint venture, and the negotiation of activities in the community, starting to recognize their potential.
3. *Active*: members are committed to developing practices and activities such as creating artifacts, and the shared repertoire adapts to changing circumstances.
4. *Dispersed*: the members no longer show a very intense commitment, but the community is still alive, demonstrated by the sharing of information and collaboration (e.g., holding meetings and calling each other to share advice).
5. *Memorable*: the community is no longer central, but members still remember it as a significant part of their identity.

Wenger and colleagues (2002) proposed the metaphor of "cultivation" to explain the process of developing communities of practice. In particular, structural elements are central to this process; they must be leveraged to grow and become, like plants, more and more "luxuriant." These elements are:

- The *thematic field* (domain): create a context and shared sense of identity, legitimizing the community by affirming its members' and other stakeholders' objectives and values.
- The *community* (community): creating the social fabric of learning. A strong community encourages interaction, sharing ideas, asking for clarification, and relationships based on mutual respect and trust; practice is that specific knowledge that communities develop, share, and maintain.

All communities of practice include these key elements, even if they take on different structures and arrangements. Continuing the biological metaphor applied to CoPs, it is stated that, like other living organisms, they go through different stages during their development, as noted below:

- *Conception phase*: the community provides for the identification of the main objectives, which must reflect the interests of individual community members and must be in line with the general purposes of the entire organization.

In addition, existing social networks are identified, and activities to support their development are carried out, identifying everyday knowledge needs.
- *Growth phase*: the community is aimed at generating a sufficient degree of energy for its development, providing for the implementation of activities that increase the awareness of everyday needs and interests, recognition of the importance of sharing knowledge concerning a specific domain, identification of what knowledge must be shared and the methods of sharing, and, finally, the development of relationships based on mutual trust.

  At this stage, trust is a fundamental factor without which community members would hardly be able to assess the most relevant elements and recognize the value of the community.
- *Maturity phase*: objectives, roles, and boundaries are further clarified, and the community aims to define the role of each within the organization and establish relationships with other areas of action. The community becomes more and more aware of itself. It focuses on managing and widening borders and achieving objectives, avoiding any "distraction" of its members, and concentrating no longer on sharing ideas and insights, but on managing and consolidating knowledge.

Specific needs and requirements may arise at each stage of a community's life cycle, precluding further development if not adequately met. Finally, the metaphor of cultivation underlines the need to feed within the community that excitement and "vitality" (aliveness) that can attract and involve its members.

Unlike teams or other structures, communities can only ensure survival through active interaction between members. In this regard, in *Cultivating Communities of Practice*, Wenger et al. suggested a design model that considers the specific nature of communities capable of fostering and evoking vitality.

This model, far from the traditional organizational design models based on the creation of structures, systems, and roles for the achievement of set objectives, is made up of seven key principles:

1. Design for evolution. According to the authors, avoid imposing a preestablished structure and let the community develop naturally.
2. Create a dialogue between internal and external perspectives.
3. Promote different levels of participation as central (core), active, or peripheral.
4. Develop public and private spaces.
5. Focus on added value.
6. Combine familiarity and excitement.
7. Create a rhythm as a specific sequence of things to do that meets the needs of all its members, making the right combination of immediate needs and prospects possible.

Earlier, Wenger (2000) identified three dimensions of community development:

1. The energy level: how a community places openness and development toward new skills and opportunities at the center of its joint enterprise.
2. The depth of social capital: the degree of sharing that supports the shared commitment to interact productively, making a mutually interconnected contribution with other community members.
3. Self-awareness: the degree to which the community is aware of the shared repertoire already developed throughout its history and its connection to its primary practices. This awareness allows the community to treat this repertoire as a dynamic element to be modified, increased, and developed.

As Wenger (1998) stated, the more these basic assumptions exist, the more participation becomes learning for all CoP members.

## Translation

In the actor-network theory (ANT), networks continuously evolve and transform through translation processes in which a temporary actor network progressively takes form, and, eventually, certain entities control others (Callon, 1986). The translation is not linear and constantly changes when it is not consistently successful.

A translation process entails four interrelated moments: problematization, interessement, enrollment, and mobilization (Callon, 1986).

In the *problematization* stage, one or more key actors attempt to frame the nature of the problem in their terms (Sarker et al., 2006); they identify and involve several actors whose roles and relationships configure an initial problem-solving network. In this stage, there is an obligatory passage point (OPP), making the actor indispensable in dealing with it (Callon, 1986).

The second stage is *interessement*. This stage embraces a group of actions by which an actor is of sufficient interest to others, so they agree with his proposal (Callon, 1986):

> Interessement is the group of actions by which an entity attempts to impose and stabilize the identity of the other actors it defines through its problematisation . . . to interest other actors is to build devices that can be placed between them and all other entities who want to define their identities otherwise. An interest's B by cutting or weakening all the links between B and the invisible (or at times quite visible) groups of other entities C, D, E, etc., who may want to link themselves to B. (Callon, 1986, pp. 207–208)

Different strategies and tactics need to be deployed for the *entity* to achieve a successful interessement, like building devices between the controlling actor and those interested. The use of representatives is another strategy in which the controlling actor negotiates interessement with those who "speak in the name of the others" (Callon, 1986, p. 214).

Interessement does not necessarily lead to successful alliances and eventually translations; enrollment needs to be reinforced (Callon, 1986). The *enrollment* process consists of "negotiations, trials of strength and tricks that accompany the interessements and enable them to succeed" (Callon, 1986, p. 211).

Finally, the last moment of translation is the *mobilization* of allies. Here the actor needs to "accumulate enough allies in one place to modify the belief and behavior of all others" (Latour, 1990, p. 60). New translation processes start to occur; however, this ordering process is never completed (Callon, 1986). A successful translation depends on how strong the cascade relationships are: "Translation continues, but the equilibrium has been modified and reality begins to fluctuate" (Callon, 1986, p. 224).

## One Concept, One Technology, and One Metaphor

### Susurration, Hybridity Possibility, and Holobiont

One concept we can rely on for collaborative development as a process is a susurration. Susurration implies the idea of a transformative accumulation of lived experiences that are in the present and quickly become the referent point for successive transformation. The human tendency to accumulate ever greater complexity is made possible by the different forms of recursion (i.e., the self-referential recursive structure of human speech that renders possible reasoning, abstraction, objectification, and subjectivation) and by how actions and speech subsume (imply) those from which they originated. Sfard (2013) used this concept to speak about the learning of mathematics. Susurration makes it possible for a process to take advantage of the past to project the future.

All of the processes analyzed to increase and develop a community could be incremented by technology, such as hybridity. Hybridity connotes the exploitation of several structures—a promising complex social space for the co-construction of knowledge, traversing physical and digital space, and using material and digital tools—for learning (Impedovo & Tan, n.d.). Technology opens new digital interaction spaces (like the Virtual World, etc.) in this hybrid reality.

The interactions of virtual and material elements are metaphorically referred to as "knots" (Gadille & Impedovo, 2019) to show the interweaving of virtuality and materiality: modality, body, settings, and resources. These knots create a zone of possibility.

Finally, the image we want to select for this chapter is the holobiont, which is an assemblage of a host and the many other species living in or around it, forming a discrete ecological unit. The components of a holobiont are individual species or bionts, and the combined genome of all points is the hologenome. The concept of the holobiont was initially defined by Lynn Margulis and René Fester in their 1991 book *Symbiosis as a Source of Evolutionary Innovation*. However, the concept has subsequently evolved from the original definition. Holobionts include the host, virome, microbiome, and other members, all of which contribute in some way to the function of the whole.

This image helps us visualize a reality between the virtual and reality, and between the individual and the social dimensions in a longitudinal perspective: growth, cycle, and translation are necessary to deal with the complexity of social learning dynamics. The pedagogical scenario itself thus becomes an extended space of possibilities that is appropriated to make it evolve in complexity.

The aspects of susurration, hybridity, possibility, and holobiont have in common a process that tries to organize itself in a new way compared to the previous modalities (linear, in presence, or unitary, and not mixed).

Students' self-organization of the learning environment is possibly not consistently implemented in the learning process. Some empirical evidence suggests that learners' autonomy is essential for academic achievement.

From this perspective, a community could self-organize learning to provide flexibility, independence, and responsibility. The role of the learning design is to support the metacognitive processes necessary for the development of the "self-determined learner" (Van Laer & Elen, 2017) and the community.

## For Learning Design

### Scripts Based on Trialogical Learning Design

Trialogical learning design (TLA) was developed by Paavola and Hakkarainen's (2021) critical principles for learning design. The six principles guide the planning of teaching and learning activities. The main characteristics of these principles focus on the mediation process, knowledge artifacts, knowledge practices, and object-oriented activities.

The appropriateness of this model is related to the extension of the innovative potential to knowledge practices, emphasizing cross-fertilization between school and community. The model is influenced by Scardamalia and Bereiter's (2003) knowledge-building theory based on collaborative learning and aimed at sustaining students in creating knowledge artifacts.

**Table 4.1. Critical Learning Design Principles**

| Six Principles | Definitions |
| --- | --- |
| *Organizing activities around shared "objects"* | Formative action is oriented to the realization of shared objects (also intended as practices and processes) recognized as essential and intended for actual use beyond the individual and social dimensions of learning. |
| *Supporting interaction between personal and social levels* | Combine individual work with collaborative work as complementary activities. |
| *Fostering long-term processes of knowledge advancement* | Introduce iterative inquiry cycles in a supportive environment, including creative reuse of previous practice and knowledge artifacts. |
| *Emphasizing development through transformation and reflection between forms of knowledge and practices* | Involve various declarative, procedural, and implicit forms of knowledge and practices. |
| *Cross-fertilization of various knowledge practices across communities and institutions* | Promote the practices and languages of different environments. |
| *Providing flexible tool mediation* | Provide adequate and diversified technologies to mediate collaborative activities. |

The model is well integrated into the literature (Lakkala et al., 2012; Rugelj & Zapušek, 2018), including engineering, technology, and digital skills (Engeness, 2021). To evaluate impact, the framework focuses on the main aspects that teacher educators could consider for successful learning design.

Paavola and Hakkarainen (2021) further identified critical learning design principles, as seen in table 4.1.

Table 4.2 presents the principles to use for a project design.

**Table 4.2. Guided Principles for a Project in TLA Perspectives**

| Principles |
| --- |
| Does your project imply the realization of a concrete object/project? Which one (e.g., a poster)? |
| In your project, how were pupils' activities planned? What about social activities? How are the two types of activities connected? |
| What kind of long-term learning for learners does your project allow? |
| Which reflective activities do you propose in your project among the different activities of knowledge and practices? |
| What activity do you propose to share with the community/institution? |
| What technological activities have you proposed to the students or implemented to realize your project? |

## TAKEAWAY IDEAS FROM THIS CHAPTER

### Reflecting on the Process of Professional Growth and Development

In this chapter, we discussed how teacher communities evolve and take different forms as well as how professional communities grow and develop to support their members. Suppose that you were wondering how to better handle classroom management issues in your first year of teaching. While discussing the topic, one of your colleagues recommended a new classroom management system that she had been using successfully in her classroom. After learning about the system, you introduced the new system to your students. However, things have gotten worse after implementing the system. You wondered what to do, and you had a chance to talk with another colleague, who invited you to observe her classes just to get hints. Observing her class opened your eyes to new ways of interacting with your students. You learned to serve as a facilitator of student learning rather than a manager. Through this experience, you learned how class observations of other classrooms could be quite informative; you also discovered the importance of talking to those colleagues who are willing to open their classrooms. You learned who to talk to for your professional growth and get hints and tips to develop your own solution. Surely every workplace has many stories like this.

Reflect on your own experiences and consider how your professional community could better help its members for professional growth and development. Again, use the theoretical frameworks just discussed as guides to consider this issue. Here are some questions to guide you in your discovery:

- What were your struggles in your first few years of teaching? What was the reason for that? Did you get any meaningful help from your colleagues then? If so, what kind of help did you get? How useful do you think it is to get connected with your colleagues for overcoming challenges and struggles in professional life?
- As is often the case in the first few years of teaching, you might have struggled with classroom management. For instance, you might have wondered why most of your students were not paying attention to you, were chatting with each other without responding to your questions, or were not following your instructions. What did you do to overcome these challenges then? What do you think you should have done instead?
- To overcome your challenges as a professional, have you consulted your colleagues for advice? If so, how helpful was the advice your colleagues gave you? Why do you feel that way?
- When you overcame the initial challenges as a first-year teacher, you might have experienced a sense of relief. You could have learned that you could continue overcoming new challenges in the same way. Based on

your experience, how would you describe the process and mechanism by which novice teachers become expert teachers? What do you think the role of your colleagues and professional community should be in the process?
- How are you now contributing to your professional community by helping novice teachers overcome challenges in their teaching? Are you directly telling them what to do? Or are you helping them construct their own solutions? What do you think is the most viable approach that works to help novice teachers grow and develop in your workplace? Are there any challenges or hurdles to implement this?
- Suppose that you realized that there were differences between you and the novice teachers you mentored, not only in teaching style but also in the goal of teaching and professional identity. How do you think it is possible to mentor them effectively if their goals and professional identities are different from yours? How do you think you should be communicating with them to support them?
- Suppose that you have had successful experiences in supporting novice teachers in your workplace. How do you think it is possible to institutionalize your approach? What does it take to implement it across the school?
- In your workplace, what kind of mentorship is taking place now? Have there been any attempts to institutionalize what is working?
- Do you have any colleagues who are your allies and whom you can easily talk to, but who are teaching different subject areas or grade levels? If so, how did you get connected with the colleagues outside your immediate teacher group? What knowledge and wisdom have the colleagues brought to you, and vice versa?
- How have you gone through the process of improving your educational practice incrementally in collaboration with your colleagues? If so, what do you feel is important to move such a collaboration forward and sustain it?
- How do those who teach different subject areas and grades communicate and support each other in your workplace? What do you think is the nature of such communications, and what are the benefits of communicating and supporting each other across different subject areas and grades? How can your school community promote such cross-sectional dialogues so that the teacher community grows and flourishes across the school?
- Can you see your teaching from the perspectives of teachers who teach your students in different subject areas or those who inherit your students at the next grade level? If so, what should be done to make the cross-sectional collaboration happen in your school for the benefit of students?
- What do you think about your organization's support system for professional development, and how is it growing now? What is missing, and what needs to be changed? What roles can technology and online space play there?

# REFERENCES

Callon, M. (1986). Some elements of a sociology of translation: Domestication of the scallops and the fishermen of St Brieuc Bay. In J. Law (Ed.), *Power, action and belief: A new sociology of knowledge?* (pp. 196–229). Routledge and Kegan Paul.

Engeness, I. (2021). Developing teachers' digital identity: towards the pedagogic design principles of digital environments to enhance students' learning in the 21st century. *European Journal of Teacher Education, 44*(1), 96–114.

Gadille, M., & Impedovo, M. A. (2019). School goes online with avatars: Extended learning in a secondary school. In *Conference on Computer Supported Collaborative Learning. Conference Proceedings* (Vol. 2, pp. 549–552).

Impedovo, M. A., & Tan, T. (n.d.). *Learning design for teacher-student co-agency in hybrid spaces* (submitted for publication 2022).

Lakkala, M., Ilomäki, L., Paavola, S., Kosonen, K., & Muukkonen, H. (2012). Using trialogical design principles to assess pedagogical practices in two higher education courses. In *Collaborative knowledge creation* (pp. 141–161). Brill.

Latour, B. (1990). Drawing things together. In M. Lynch & S. Woolgar (Eds.), *Representation in scientific practice* (pp. 19–68). MIT Press.

Levine, J. M., & Moreland, R. L. (1994). Group socialization: Theory and research. *European Review of Social Psychology, 5*(1), 305–336.

Margulis, L., & Fester, R. (Eds.). (1991). *Symbiosis as a source of evolutionary innovation: Speciation and morphogenesis.* MIT Press.

McMurrain, T. T., & Gazda, G. M. (1974). Extended group interaction: Interpersonal functioning as a developmental process variable. *Small Group Behaviour, 5,* 393–404.

Paavola, S., & Hakkarainen, K. (2021). Trialogical learning and object-oriented collaboration. In U. Cress, C. P. Rosé, A. F. Wise, & J. Oshima (Eds.), *International handbook of computer-supported collaborative learning* (241–259). Springer.

Rugelj, J., & Zapušek, M. (2018). Innovative and flexible forms of teaching and learning with information and communication technologies. National Conference on Education and Research in the Information Society. Plovdiv, Bulgaria. http://hdl.handle.net/10525/2942

Sarker, S., Sarker, S., & Sidorova, A. (2006). Understanding business process change failure: An actor-network perspective. *Journal of Management Information Systems, 23*(1), 51–86.

Scardamalia, M., & Bereiter, C. (2003). Knowledge building environments: Extending the limits of the possible in education and knowledge work. In G. D. Jaynes (Ed.), *Encyclopedia of distributed learning* (pp. 269–272). SAGE.

Sfard, A. (2013). Commentary: On metaphorical roots of conceptual growth. In *Mathematical reasoning* (pp. 347–380). Routledge.

Tuckman, B. W. (1965). Developmental sequence in small groups. *Psychological Bulletin, 63,* 384–399.

Van Laer, S., & Elen, J. (2017). In search of attributes that support self-regulation in blended learning environments. *Education and Information Technologies, 22,* 1395–1454.

Wenger, E. (1998). Communities of practice: Learning as a social system. *Systems Thinker,* 9(5), 2–3.

Wenger, E. (2000). Communities of practice and social learning systems. *The Organization,* 7(2), 225–246.

Wenger, E., McDermott, R., & Snyder, W. M. (2002). *Cultivating communities of practice: A guide to managing knowledge.* Harvard Business School.

Worchel, S., Grossman, M., & Countat-Sassic, D. (1991). L'influenza minoritaria nel contest gruppale: come i fattori di gruppo agiscono sull'influenza della minoranza. *Ricerche di Psicologia, 4,* 125–145.

*Chapter Five*

# How to Connect in a Teacher Community

> These are types of teaching that organize the fundamental ways in which future practitioners are educated for their new professions. In these signature pedagogies, the novices are instructed in critical aspects of the three fundamental dimensions of professional work—to think, to perform, and to act with integrity. —L. S. Shulman (2005)

In the previous chapters, we examined and analyzed teacher community dynamics from constitution to entry into and development of the group. In this section, we focus on the exchange elements that the community can activate to build knowledge, products, and new processes.

## THREE PERSPECTIVES

Below, we consider three perspectives: *resources*, *repertoires*, and *lines*.

### Resources

Norms are scales of values that define shared expectations of group members' behavior (Levine & Moreland, 1990). Being a collective product, they include rules of behavior and relate to expressive methods (such as linguistic jargon, clothing, and the common cult of shared aspects), sometimes incomprehensible to external observers.

According to Sherif (1967), together with structure, norms constitute the essence of the group itself: social situations that lack these properties cannot be defined as groups but rather as mere aggregates. As for peripheral norms, low-status members are sanctioned more frequently than "superiors" if they violate peripheral standards. The latter are freer not to adhere to peripheral norms; they can even change them. High-status members are more obliged than others to guarantee compliance because the group's survival and their authority depend on them. Therefore, each norm has its own "breadth of acceptance" (Sherif & Sherif, 1969), understood as the range of "acceptable" behaviors that can be salient and depend on the member's position within the group.

Bettenhausen and Murnighan (1985) underlined the cognitive matrix of norms resulting from negotiations between group members. The speed of development of the rules and the number of negotiations depend on how much the members share the same scripts and the homogeneity in categorizing the various experiences. According to Cartwright and Zander (1968), the construction of group norms could have four functions:

1. The advancement of the group toward its objectives: in case of conflict, the rules can become more rigid and constructive to close ranks and increase internal cohesion.
2. The maintenance of the group: that is, the rules allow the group to preserve itself as such against its extinction.
3. The construction of social reality: built on an intersubjective basis and maintained through social pressures that push toward uniformity. The rules make it possible to maintain a shared conception of reality, serving as a reference point for members' self-assessment.
4. The definition of the group's relations with the social environment: this makes it possible to classify external groups as friends and enemies.

At an individual level, the functions of these norms become filters through which to interpret the world, provide order and predictability to events, and give indications on the behavior to be implemented in a new or ambiguous situation.

In formal groups with a long history, norms usually preexist. At a social level, they regulate social existence and, consequently, help coordinate the activities of group members and can improve the group's identity. The individual who enters the group is strongly influenced by the group regulations and must adapt to them to survive. Another function of the norm, according to Moscovici (1972), is the avoidance of conflict.

The variety of individual judgments can prevent agreement, generating competing opinions. According to Moscovici (1972), a group rule arises thanks to negotiations that lead to convergent evaluations, avoiding conflict. Another factor to consider is the temporal one: the rules can vary according to the different circumstances the group has to face (consolidation, confrontation with external groups, internal crises, etc.).

The role is defined as the set of exhibited and expected behaviors of the various components. An example is Zimbardo's (1972) famous study, conducted in the basement of Stanford University. The study was designed to examine the effects of situational variables on participants' reactions and behaviors in a two-week simulation of a prison environment. According to Brown (1989), roles fulfill the function of:

- facilitating the achievement of the group's purpose;
- bringing order to the group's existence: we have different expectations from different roles and relate differently; and
- contributing to our self-definition, to the awareness of what we are.

Roles allow a predictable and orderly group to achieve group goals. According to Levine and Moreland (1990), in almost all groups, it is possible to distinguish four roles:

1. Leader: stands at the top of the status hierarchy and has a central function to which all members refer (for further details, see the chapter on leadership).
2. Newcomer: neophyte who has recently arrived in the group. She exhibits caution and circumspection because she must understand the implicit and explicit rules of entering the environment.
3. Scapegoat: this is a rather uncomfortable role for those who play it as it continually attracts criticism and disapproval, showing themselves inadequately, expressing fears and hesitations, judged out of place. The scapegoat has a "protective" function in the group, allowing other members to project the negative parts of the self-image.
4. Clown: plays a socioemotional role in relieving inevitable tensions in the group.

In addition to these four figures, according to some scholars, is the "opposition leader," who is understood as the one who creates dissent in the group.

Conflicts can arise in assigning roles, and members may disagree about how a position/role should be played. Conflicts can arise on an individual level when a person begins to play a role and then loses motivation and skills or becomes aware that it is an inconsistent role with the parts that he already plays. Role conflicts in workgroups increase tensions and bring about a decrease in productivity.

## Repertoires

Wenger (1998) includes in the shared repertoire "routines, words, tools, ways of operating, stories, gestures, symbols, genres (styles), actions or concepts" (p. 98) that the community has produced or adopted during its existence and that have become part of its practices: it is the entire repertoire of shared meanings that allows social interaction and the development of the practice. The objects produced can be texts, hypertexts, websites, projects or programs, theoretical elaborations, problem solutions, and the definition of principles.

These repertoires are inherently ambiguous: they do not have a fixed meaning but are linked to the continuous negotiation processes implemented within the CoP. This ambiguity constitutes the intrinsic condition for creating new meanings, reified through the production of new objects (mental and physical) and new procedures (interaction between the participants, the timing). This process is beneficial for new community members who are involved in an increasingly broader path of participation, to the point of helping to modify the available repertoire itself.

In this way, it is possible to expand and renew the community's shared repertoire, which serves as a basis for subsequent negotiations. Thus, meanings and interpretations settled over time represent a resource for producing new meanings, making innovation, and realizing increasingly complex forms of possible activities (Wenger, 1998): "material realizations tend to perpetuate repertoires of practices beyond the circumstances that generated them" (p. 107).

An element of connection with the outside is represented for Wenger by intermediation factors, which play an essential role in introducing new elements to practice. In this gluing process, we find the position of intermediaries, who, as Wenger (2011) stated, "can create new connections between communities of practice, to facilitate coordination and—if they are good mediators—to open new possibilities of meaning" (p. 128).

The meaning of language derives from its social use: "nothing is real if there is no social agreement that it is" (Gergen, 1988, p. 8). The agreement is based on both innovations and negotiations of meaning, and in dialogue; one receives the privilege of purpose from others.

The relationship between communication and intersubjectivity is closely interconnected. Merleau-Ponty (1965) had the merit of emphasizing the importance of communication through which intersubjectivity is manifested: dialogue becomes a common platform between the other and me. The intersubjective process is a state in which two or more interacting people can reach mutual understanding thanks to sharing the meanings and purposes of the interaction (Rommetveit, 1974).

Intersubjectivity and communication were the subjects of a study by Wells (1990), who described intersubjectivity as a multidimensional phenomenon. The intersubjective condition can be understood as a situation in which the students reach an agreement about

- the object of learning,
- the specific objective of the learning activity,
- the meaning that the object of learning has for the community, and
- acceptance and mutual respect for the other's opinion.

Meaning is mediated until an ordinary meaning is shared.

In digital communication environments, the intersubjective dimension assumes even more relevance: a proliferation of opportunities to meet other subjects with different cultures and points of view, allowing a continuous redefinition of the self and the acquisition of new positions (Hermans et al., 1992).

## Lines

The theoretical lens of the actor-network theory (ANT) is used to understand the link between humans and nonhumans in a complex configuration. For example, studying the adoption of technologies could be appropriate to use this perspective, dealing with a wide range of information technologies such as intranet, geographical information systems, and enterprise resource planning systems.

It could be interesting to deal with how human and nonhuman actors persuade each other to align their interests toward a common goal. The existence of powerful actors whose strategies can mobilize other actors is required to accept new technologies (Linde et al., 2003). The actors could develop specific relations and embrace certain strategies to hold together long enough to achieve a particular purpose—to become a stable actor network, a technology used in practice.

Human actors (e.g., project leaders, senior sponsors, "ordinary staff") and nonhuman actors (e.g., documents, policies, instructions, concepts, technology artifacts such as the online community and its constituent components)—both internal and external to a particular network—must be given relevant attention when looking at the adoption of technologies, to retrace lines and connections. Also, ANT can be used as a framework to enhance understanding online community participation. The analysis of existing studies shows how those supporting the adoption of technologies (e.g., technologies supporting online communities) may not command sufficient social and political power within the organization to motivate its widespread adoption. A fragmented actor network supporting the adoption of collaborative technology might find it difficult to sustain its position when its staff has effectively joined competing networks or created new ones (Hall & Goody, 2007, p. 186).

This section has analyzed three main elements: repertoires, connections, and lines. The three elements help to think about the learning dynamics of the teacher community from an interactive perspective.

## One Concept, One Technology, and One Metaphor

### Extended Cognition, AI, and Rhizome

The three proposed concepts of *extended cognition*, *artificial intelligence*, and *rhizome* have in common a dimension of extension in space and time, invading new spaces and seeking opportunities for extension.

The concept of "distributed cognition" proposes expanding the concept of "situated cognition" as it considers all the material and intangible components of the environment in which learning takes place.

Metaphorically, knowledge is no longer localized in a single person's mind. Hutchins (1995; 2001) has developed the idea of distributed cognition since the mid-1980s. The concept explains the complexity of knowledge construction processes because the interpretation provided by conventional approaches, according to which they are comparable to individual processes, is considered insufficient.

The distributed cognition approach emphasizes the "distributed" nature in time and space of the phenomena of cognition. It extends the scope of what is considered cognitive beyond the single individual, reconnecting the activity of thinking with the resources and materials in the social and cultural context.

Intuitively, we can approach distributed cognition with artificial intelligence (AI) as an example of a system that surrounds us and claims to be in connection with our minds to observe and learn from the global context in which it acts. According to the artificial intelligence market in the U.S. Education Sector report, artificial intelligence in U.S. education was expected to grow by 47.5% from 2017 to 2021. Teachers and AI are already collaborating to help develop skills and testing systems. The COVID-19 pandemic has shown the application, platforms, and tech solutionism model of teaching and learning. The field is oriented to automate administrative tasks, and new solutions are coming. A positivist vision claims a relationship between AI and education, oriented to the best for the students. A more pessimistic vision predicts the domination of the artificial intelligence system in our choices and future possibilities.

The rhizome is a philosophical concept that describes systems with no clear beginning or end, such as the internet. The term was developed by Gilles Deleuze and Félix Guattari in their capitalism and schizophrenia (1972–1980) project. Deleuze talked about an "image of thought" that apprehends multiplicities based on the botanical rhizome. Deleuze and Guattari used the terms "rhizome" and "rhizomatic" (from Ancient Greek ῥίζωμα, *rhízōma*, "mass of roots") to describe theory and research that allows for multiple, nonhierarchical entry and exit points in data representation and interpretation.

Their famous book *A Thousand Plateaus* opposed an arborescent (hierarchic, treelike) conception of knowledge, with dualist categories and binary choices. A rhizome works with planar and trans-species connections; an arborescent model works with vertical and linear connections. Their use of "the orchid and the wasp" was taken from the biological concept of mutualism. Two different species interact together to form a diversity (i.e., a unity that is multiple in itself). Hybridization or horizontal gene transfer would also be good illustrations.

The rhizome resists the organizational structure of the root-tree system, which charts causality along chronological lines and looks for the source of "things" and toward the pinnacle or conclusion of those "things." A rhizome, on the other hand,

> ceaselessly establishes connections between semiotic chains, organizations of power, and circumstances relative to the arts, sciences, and social struggles. A semiotic chain is like a tuber agglomerating very diverse acts, both linguistic and perceptive, mimetic, gestural, and cognitive. (p. 7)

Rather than narrativize history and culture, the rhizome presents history and culture as a map or wide array of attractions and influences with no specific origin or genesis, for a rhizome has no beginning or end; it is always in the middle, between things, interbeing, *intermezzo*. The rhizome's planar movement resists chronology and organization, favoring a nomadic growth and propagation system.

Applying these three concepts to the group, community, and network extension phase means having in mind the possibility of the group seeking resources elsewhere to support the training enrichment effort and, at the same time, thinking about the structure of the training process.

The individual and the community carry out this process spontaneously, interacting with other social groups and looking for links and resources in the virtual and in the following contexts. The training project and environments must leave room for growth and expansion, with a partial loss of control and dominance over the process.

## For Learning Design

### Virtual Exchange

Teacher education institutions need to increase openness in cross-national and cross-institutional collaboration resulting from international processes (Goodwin, 2020). For mutual enrichment, teachers could take advantage of innovative, intercultural, and international collaboration (Oolbekkink-Marchand et al., 2017), triggering negotiation of processes, knowledge, resources, and new modality action.

The professional development of teacher-students can benefit from an international orientation through, for example, professional mobility and the opening up of shared spaces for intercultural dialogue. The European Commission has included virtual mobility in its initiatives (see Erasmus+ Programme Guide 2019, 2020) as a modern and innovative type of education (Bruhn-Zass, 2017).

Virtual mobility has started as a complement to physical mobility, and now it is a critical trend of collaboration development between higher education institutions (HEIs). Virtual mobility has been defined according to different stages of development, organizational framework, actors involved, and technologies used (Iucu et al., 2022). It is defined as:

> Virtual exchange involves the engagement of groups of learners in *extended periods of online intercultural interaction and collaboration with partners from other cultural contexts or geographical locations as an integrated part of their educational programs* and under the guidance of educators and expert facilitators. (O'Dowd, 2018, p. 5)

The main dimensions to consider in the design are partnerships, tasks, technology, mentoring and support, integration, and recognition (The EVALUATE Group, 2019).

The new Erasmus+ Programme 2021–2027 talks about the blended intensive program (BIP) as this would join HEIs in at least three program countries, where learners come together. The learners can be either students or staff who attend training activities, including physical activity and an online component. The BIP should foster the development of transnational and transdisciplinary curricula, innovative ways of learning and teaching online collaboration, research-based learning, and challenge-based approaches that tackle societal challenges.

## TAKEAWAY IDEAS FROM THIS CHAPTER

### Reflecting on Knowledge Creation in Teacher Communities

In this chapter, we discussed how different conditions of professional community define the nature of teacher communities. Particularly, various forms of norms, rules, and routines in a workplace could heavily influence the ways members of a professional community interact and co-construct knowledge. This is a very important issue for nurturing and sustaining a professional teacher community.

However, norms, rules, and routines may not be clearly visible or stipulated in written documents, electronic texts, or other forms. They may be implicitly shared as the members of the community communicate about them through informal dialogues or co-experiences in the workplace over the years. Without considering this issue, everything you do in your professional community could be out of context. No matter how wonderful your ideas are, if you do not consider how norms, rules, and routines work, your attempts to co-construct new knowledge and skills in a teacher community are not likely to work in the context. Therefore, it is essential to reflect on both visible and invisible norms, rules, and routines that can affect the ways things are handled and knowledge is constructed in your professional community.

Especially for newcomers, this issue is crucial. Implicitly shared norms, rules, and routines could be one of the main sources of their frustrations or confusions at the workplace. Many experienced members of a professional community must have acquired and internalized implicitly shared norms, rules, and routines, but newcomers need to engage in a task to figure them out and make sense of them. Also, newcomers can be at risk of being seen as immature by other community members if their communication and behavior deviate from implicitly shared norms, rules, and routines. This can be quite frustrating for them, and it can serve as a large obstacle for the development of a teacher community.

As a member of your professional community, you might have witnessed many such cases where implicitly shared norms, rules, and routines hamper the attempts of the teacher community to co-construct new knowledge and skills. Or you might have witnessed implicitly shared norms, rules, and routines supporting the attempts to co-construct new knowledge and skills. Reflect on the following issues by making use of the theoretical frameworks discussed above and create your own takeaways. Here are some guiding questions:

- What norms, rules, and routines exist and influence your teaching in your professional community? What part of these is not clearly visible or explicitly written? For instance, how specifically are the instructional procedures defined, and how explicitly does the curriculum show what to cover on each day in your classes? How clearly are the procedures for decision making in teacher meetings defined? In what documents is this stipulated, if at all? Where do the procedures come from, and what kinds of influence do they have on educational practice at your school?

- In your professional community, what norms, rules, and routines are beneficial for co-construction of knowledge and educational practice improvement? What norms, rules, and routines are harmful? What kinds of effects do they have on the teacher communities in your workplace? What defines whether norms, rules, and routines are beneficial or harmful? What could be done to eliminate harmful norms, rules, and routines?
- In your professional community, who defines the norms, rules, and routines? What do you think about the ways they are defined? For instance, how are teacher meetings structured? Who plays leadership roles and influences the ways the members of your professional community make decisions, codevelop, and share knowledge? How do you feel about this?
- For instance, you may see your leadership team (i.e., principal, directors, chairpersons, etc.) play key roles in defining the norms, rules, and routines in your school. Their roles may constitute an integral part of daily educational practice and the ways decisions are made in your professional community. How do you see their influence on the norms, rules, and routines in your workplace?
- How did the norms, rules, and routines change in your community over the years? And how did they get changed? For instance, you and your colleagues may not like the procedure through which teachers in your school are assigned to different academic classes. What is the process to change the procedure in your workplace? How democratic do you think the change process is? If not, what kind of change is needed?
- What do you see as the role that you play in your teacher community based on Levine and Moreland's 1990 framework discussed above—that is, leader, newcomer, scapegoat, and clown? How do you feel about it? What role would you like to play in the future, and what do you think you should do to implement this?
- How are intersubjective dialogues among the members of your professional community promoted or hindered by the existing community norms, rules, and routines? How can the situation be improved? What does it take for you and your colleagues to get connected and to share honest feelings, reflections, and personal ideas with each other in your professional community?
- COVID-19 must have drastically changed the norms, rules, and routines in your professional community. What changes were brought about during

the COVID-19 crisis? Which ones are positive? Which ones are negative? What is needed to undo and overcome the negative changes?
- What do you think are the new norms, rules, and routines brought by online technology in the post-COVID era? What kinds of dialogues among the members of the professional community are done to mindfully embrace all the changes and ensure the quality of teacher communities in your workplace? If not, what should be done to action such dialogues?

## REFERENCES

Bettenhausen, K., & Murnighan, J. K. (1985). The emergence of norms in competitive decision-making groups. *Administrative Science Quarterly*, 350–372.

Brown, R. (1989). *Group processes: Dynamics within and between groups*. Basil Blackwell.

Bruhn-Zass, E. (2017). Towards a framework for virtual internationalisation. *International Journal of E-Learning & Distance Education, 32*(1).

Cartwright, D., & Zander, A. (Eds.). (1968). *Group dynamics: Research and theory* (3rd ed.). Harper & Row.

Deleuze, G., & Guattari, F. (1980). *A thousand plateaus* (B. Massumi, Trans.). University of Minnesota Press.

Erasmus+. (2019). *Erasmus+ Programme Guide 2019*. https://agence.erasmusplus.fr/programme-erasmus/presentation-programme-erasmus/le-guide-du-programme

Erasmus+. (2020). *Erasmus+ Programme Guide 2020*. https://agence.erasmusplus.fr/programme-erasmus/presentation-programme-erasmus/le-guide-du-programme

European Commission. (2021). Erasmus+ Programme Guide. https://erasmus-plus.ec.europa.eu/document/erasmus-programme-guide-2021

The EVALUATE Group. (2019). Evaluating the impact of virtual exchange on initial teacher education: A European policy experiment. Research-publishing.net. https://doi.org/10.14705/rpnet.2019.29.9782490057337

Gergen, K. J. (1988). Narrative and self as the relationship. In L. Berkowitz (Ed.), *Advances in experimental social psychology* (vol. 21, pp. 17–56). Academic Press.

Goodwin, A. L. (2020). Globalization, global mindsets and teacher education. *Action in Teacher Education, 42*(1), 6–18.

Hall, H., & Goody, M. (2007). KM, culture and compromise: Interventions to promote knowledge sharing supported by technology in corporate environments. *Journal of Information Science, 33*(2), 181–188.

Hermans, H. J. M., Kempen, H. J. G., & Van Loon, R. J. P. (1992). The dialogical self: Beyond individualism and rationalism. *American Psychologist, 47*(1), 23–33.

Hutchins, E. (1995). *Cognition in the wild*. MIT Press.

Hutchins, E. (2001). Distributed cognition. In N. J. Smelser & P. B. Baltes (Eds.), *International encyclopedia of the social and behavioral sciences* (pp. 2068–2072). Elsevier Science.

Iucu, R., Ciolan, L., Nedelcu, A., Zus, R., Dumitrache, A., Cartis, A., Vennarini, L., Fernandez de Pinedo, N., & Pericica, A. (2022). Digitally enhanced mobility. *CIVIS handbook on virtual mobility*. https://civis.eu/storage/files/civis-virtual-mobility-handbook.pdf

Levine, J. M., & Moreland, R. L. (1990). Progress in small group research. *Annual Review of Psychology, 41*, 583–634.

Linde, A., Linderoth, H., & Raisanen, C. (2003). An actor network theory perspective on IT-projects: A battle of wills. *Action in Language, Organizations and Information Systems*, 237–250.

Merleau-Ponty, M. (1965). *Fenomenologia della percezione*. Il Saggiatore.

Moscovici, S. (1972). Theory and society in social psychology. In J. Israel & H. Tajfel (Eds.), *The context of social psychology: A critical assessment*. Academic Press.

O'Dowd, R. (2018). From telecollaboration to virtual exchange: State-of-the-art and the role of UNICollaboration in moving forward. *Research-publishing.net, 1*, 1–23.

O'Dowd, R. (2020). A transnational model of virtual exchange for global citizenship education. *Language Teaching, 53*(4), 477–490. https://doi.org/10.1017/S0261444819000077

Oolbekkink-Marchand, H. W., Hadar, L. L., Smith, K., Helleve, I., & Ulvik, M. (2017). Teachers' perceived professional space and their agency. *Teaching and Teacher Education, 62*, 37–46.

Rommetveit, R. (1974). *On message structure: A framework for the study of language and communication*. Wiley.

Sherif, M. (1967). *Social interaction, process and products*. Aldine.

Sherif, M., & Sherif, C. W. (1969). *Groups in harmony and tension: An integration of studies on intergroup relations*. Octagon Books.

Shulman, L. S. (2005). Signature pedagogies in the professions. *Daedalus, 134*(3), 52–59.

Wells, G. (1990). Talk about text: Where literacy is learned and taught. *Curriculum Inquiry, 20*(4), 369–405.

Wenger, E. (1998). *Communities of practice: Learning, meaning and identity*. Cambridge University Press.

Wenger, E. (2011). Communities of practice: A brief introduction. University of Oregon Scholars' Bank. https://scholarsbank.uoregon.edu/xmlui/bitstream/handle/1794/11736/A%20brief%20introduction%20to%20CoP.pdf?sequence=1&isAllowed=y

Zimbardo, P. G. (1972). Comment: Pathology of imprisonment. *Society, 9*(6), 4–8.

## Chapter Six

# Expanding a Teacher Community

Don't try to preach something to your audience, rather give them situations and let them decide for themselves. —C. Zhao (in Hellerman, 2021)

After the processes proposed in the previous chapters, the intention here is to talk about the expansion of a teacher community. Below, three approaches are discussed.

## THREE PERSPECTIVES FOR EXPANSION OF A TEACHER COMMUNITY

In this section, we analyze *status*, *engagement*, and *multi-experience*.

### Status

Group members enjoy different power and prestige that give rise to status hierarchies, differentiating the members from each other. The concept of "status" refers to an individual's position in a group and evaluating this position on a prestige scale.

The status system is considered the general pattern of social influence among group members (Levine & Moreland, 1990). Status is an essential structural and stable aspect that characterizes a group. Formal and informal hierarchies of power and popularity are often identifiable in each group, even by observing nonverbal behavior. If the roles help us understand who we are, status differentiation helps us understand competence through social comparison.

According to Festinger (1957), there is a universal human motivation to compare and evaluate our opinions and capabilities through social confrontation. Generally, to obtain a reliable and reassuring evaluation, we tend to choose individuals just a little better than we are as a term of comparison. Higher ratings are uncomfortable, and, in some circumstances, comparisons are made downward (e.g., when they are in significantly adverse conditions). Also, the group's performance tends to decline if there is too much homogeneity or discrepancy.

The leader is at the top of the prestige ladder in a group. He is defined as "the person who can influence other members of a group more than he is himself influenced" (Brown, 1989). From the early 1900s to the present day, there have been several experimental studies and theories on leadership, each with a different definition of leadership.

In this theoretical evolution, we speak of transformational leadership, which falls within the "new leadership" paradigms. This theory is linked to empowerment, where the leader is the "one who can encourage his collaborators to do more than what they originally expected to do" (Bass, 1985, p. 20). A fundamental element is the importance of the participants in the leadership process, which involves the interaction among leaders, followers, and situations.

Bass (1985) proposed a leadership theory as a continuum that goes from the transformational and transactional styles to a style of nonleadership (i.e., when the leader fails in his role, does not provide feedback, or does not meet the needs of his subordinates). The transformational style involves four factors or dimensions known as the "four I's":

1. *Idealized* influence: the transformational leader implements behaviors that make them role models for their collaborators.
2. *Inspirational* motivation: the transformational leader motivates collaborators, involving them in attractive situations.
3. *Intellectual* stimulation: the transformational leader stimulates followers to be effective, creative, and innovative.
4. *Individualized* consideration: the transformational leader is attentive to each follower's needs for growth and success.

Transformational leadership comes closest to the leadership process seen as the distribution of social power and shared responsibility within a group. The strengths of the transformational theory include the interactive process that involves both the leader's and the followers' needs; the group members, therefore, recognize their own needs and collaborate to improve individuals and the group.

Finally, charismatic leadership is considered similar to transformational leadership, emphasizing the leader as an agent of change. It takes up the Christian concept of charisma as a gift bestowed on others (House, 1976). It can be seen that charismatic leadership is firmly based on value systems and ideology, arousing expectation and deep trust of the followers in the leader's abilities.

Group cohesion can be defined as "the cement that holds group members together and maintains their mutual relationships" (Schachter et al., 1951, p. 229). Festinger (1957) considers that two forces act on the members of a group and determine group cohesion:

1. group attraction: refers to the desire of individuals to have interpersonal interactions with other group members and the desire to be involved in group activities, and
2. control of means: concerns the benefits a group member derives from being part of a group.

Hogg (1992) defined group cohesion as the attraction of the members to the idea of the group and its prototypical image. The group is cohesive when its members identify with the characteristics and ideals that distinguish it from other groups. Cohesion, defined as interpersonal attraction, includes physical proximity, task orientation, similarity, and uniformity of opinion.

The concept of cohesion based solely on interpersonal attraction was considered reductive. For this reason, a more elaborate definition of cohesion has been developed, understood as a social attraction that considers the theory of the social identity of Tajfel (1981) and the theory of the categorization of the self by Turner (1987). In this meaning, cohesion is the tendency to be reflected in the characteristics that identify the group, not the individual members. Other factors include intergroup conflict, which refers to competition and discrimination of the outgroup and performance.

Cohesion also positively affects the group because it can favor the sharing of knowledge. In a cohesive group, the knowledge and skills of each member can be integrated with those of the others, and all members can benefit from all the information and experiences gained by others. The positive value of cohesion is especially evident when the group faces difficult moments and complex situations.

In summary, group cohesion is a multidimensional concept (several factors are linked to whether a group is united, such as social, task-related, and personal aspects); dynamic (the cohesion of a group can change over time); instrumental (groups are created for a purpose, and cohesion facilitates their achievement); and with good connotations (the social interactions of the members of a group create emotional and affective states between them).

The relationship between groups is crucial for understanding social reality, considering continuous confrontation, conflict, and collaboration. According to Tajfel (1981), the effects of categorization lead to favoritism for one's group. When there are two groups and the subject is inside one and outside another, favoritism is created for the in-group and discrimination for the out-group. Tajfel argued that in-group favoritism and out-group discrimination were determined by categorization. Social confrontation activates the group members' need for positive specificity toward the out-group.

Turner (1987) considered the self-categorization theory (SCT) as one of the most exciting developments of the social identity theory (SIT). Unlike the theory of social identity, according to which social identity derives from group membership, in the view of self-categorization, social identity constitutes a level of abstraction of the cognitive representation of one's self.

The SCT tries to clarify how people conceptualize themselves as belonging to specific social categories. It considers individual and group behavior as "acting in terms of the self" but of a self that operates at different levels of abstraction. People can use different levels of abstraction when categorizing themselves and others. The cognitive process of categorization involves an accentuation of intra-category similarities and inter-category differences. The three levels of self-abstraction are:

1. The *superordinate level* in which the subject sees himself (himself) as a human being considers those elements of a more general nature (human identity).
2. The *intermediate level* is where the subject (the self) sees itself as a member of one group compared to other members (social identity).
3. The *subordinate level* is where the individual (the self) sees the self as a unique entity concerning the other members of the in-group (personal identity).

Such studies are central to understanding prejudices and stereotypes, the subject of extensive treatment in social psychology. Finally, we recall the contribution of Brown (1995), who, starting from the critical contribution of Tajfel, highlighted the cognitive aspects of prejudice and underlined its emotional aspects and possible behavioral expressions.

Prejudice, therefore, must be studied as a group phenomenon because it represents complex categories of people rather than isolated individuals; it is a socially shared orientation. It is a function of the relationship between the group that expresses it and the out-group.

Collective effectiveness can be defined as Bandura (2003) did: "the shared belief of a group regarding the joint ability to organize and execute the courses of action necessary to achieve objectives of various levels" (p. 639). The most recent research on collective self-efficacy (Bandura, 2003) has shown that it is positively correlated with perceptions of group cohesion (Paskevich et al., 2001).

The sense of personal and collective effectiveness differs in the subject exercising the faculty to produce effects. Still, the two types of belief in effectiveness have similar sources, functions, and processes. The sense of collective effectiveness affects the kind of future that the members of a group seek to achieve, the way they manage their resources, the plans and strategies they develop, the amount of commitment they invest in groups, the resistance that exists to situations where collective efforts do not produce quick results or meet stubborn opponents, and the collaboration within the group.

The concept of cohesion overlaps and fades with the sense of community. The most exhaustive model of the sense of community was developed by McMillan and Chavis (1986), who highlighted the construct of the sense of community based on four interdependent dimensions:

1. Belonging is linked to membership and refers to investing part of oneself to become a group member. It includes sub-dimensions that help define who is part of the community and who is not: borders (some people are part of the community and others are not), emotional security, sense of belonging and identification, personal investment, symbolic system.
2. Reciprocal member-group influence leads to a process of identification in the group and a willingness to sacrifice oneself for the group.
3. Integration and satisfaction of needs, concerning the effort that brings one to feel part of the community: the sense of community is nourished by the perception of being in a competent group and knowing whose competence one can benefit from.
4. Emotional sharing: personal investment leads to perceiving the group as significant and establishing an emotional bond with it, including as sub-dimensions: contacts, quality of interaction, shared experience, sharing of salient events, emotional investment, effects of honors and humiliation, as well as spiritual bond.

A model that considers contradictions as central is the expanding learning model or the model of knowledge expansion, sharing the spirit of innovation and renewal. This model has Finnish scholar Engeström (1999) as its leading representative; it is part of the theory of activity (TA).

At the basis of the theory, the social and historical-cultural dimension is central to developing human psychic structures. Initially identified in a single individual, the learner gradually becomes a broader subject, coinciding with entire collective forms and networks of systems. The original view gave birth to three successive generations, as many enriched the first theoretical framework.

## Engagement

According to Wenger (1998), each community of practice is built through the mutual commitment of its members, who interact with each other and establish rules and relationships of mutuality, polarizing their activity. Sharing the same commitment with others and organizing one's functional interactions around this mutual commitment allows the existence of the CoP much more than sharing a specific physical characteristic or being united by spatial proximity.

The creation of a mutual commitment is based on codified dynamics (such as working in the same place and exchanging information) and, above all, through continuous informal processes of exchange and sharing. Wenger (1998) identified three constitutive mechanisms of mutual commitment:

1. Cooperative work: carrying out an activity aimed at the realization of a product or service, the solution of a problem, or, in general, the execution of a task.
2. Diversity and partiality: the work of each group member implies a positive interdependence with the work of other members and is part of a complex organization that does not, however, lead to homogenization in participation.
3. Mutual relationships: involvement in practice implies a joint commitment among members through the development of relationships.

Each group member's work implies a positive interdependence with the work of other members. Indeed, what makes engagement in a community possible is precisely the diversity produced by the division of roles and functions. Each participant holds a unique place and develops an exclusive identity defined and integrated during participation. The identities of the various participants are interconnected by joint commitment without merging (Wenger, 1998).

Involvement in practice means mutual commitment among the members by developing functional relationships to grow individual skills. According to Wenger (1998), even rebellion reveals a more significant commitment than passive conformism as a form of participation.

Leadership is defined as distributed (Lumsden & Lumsden, 1996) when the rotation of the leadership role is attributed based on the specific skills required at particular moments in group life. From a more contemporary perspective, leadership influences relationships between leaders and collaborators, promoting fundamental changes reflecting mutual goals (Rost, 1991, p. 102). It follows that everyone contributes to the cocreation of knowledge in the group's problem-solving processes. Johnson and Johnson (1991) proposed the following definition:

> Leadership is a set of learned skills that everyone with a minimum of skills can acquire. Responsible participation in the group and leadership depend on flexible behavior, the ability to diagnose which actions are needed at a particular time for the group to function effectively, and the ability to fulfill these behaviors or get others to achieve them.
>
> Therefore, a skilled member or leader must be able to see if a given function is needed in a group and must be able to adapt sufficiently to provide the different types of behavior required for different situations. Also, an influential group member or leader should be able to use the skills of other group members to provide necessary actions for the group. (p. 65)

Group participation and leadership depend on effective behavior and the ability to diagnose actions helpful in satisfying the group's needs. Therefore, leadership does not consist of entrusting the responsibility of leading the group to a single member but in a set of behaviors or roles that all group members can activate or acquire.

Lipnack and Stamps (1997) spoke of shared leadership based on the same motivations. In the first case, the delineation of a group culture occurs, which becomes stronger the more experiences are shared. It is achieved through the continuous influence of the leader on the followers, which can be expressed through successes and failures.

Van Loon (2013) proposed the concept of a "dialogic leader" who can choose between different positions: the entrepreneur, the manager, and the coach. The dialogic leader lets one of these positions become more salient depending on the needs and objectives of the group but also based on his own past experiences, relegating the rest to the background. If this leader then finds himself working in an intercultural context, he will have to, through a transfer from one position to another, use a position already known in a new culture, overcoming problems of adaptation and taking action for new challenges.

According to Isaacs (1999), the dialogic leader is one who, through conversation, reveals the hidden meaning of each situation. We identify four skills to support this process: arouse people's sincere opinion, listen deeply, respect and give legitimate credibility to points of view, and broaden perspective and awareness. For teachers—as the leader in a dialogical position—the communication is oriented to an effective learning output.

## Multi-experience

ANT proposes the principle of general symmetry that ascribes agency to human and nonhuman actors. The basis of this principle argues that humans and nonhumans must be seen as active entities. Accordingly, technologies must not be seen as neutral or inert but as actors that cannot be taken for granted. This discussible principal position of ANT seeks to overcome the overemphasis on human agency. Latour (1991) responded:

> We are left with the accusation of immorality, apoliticism, or moral relativism. ... [However] to make a diagnosis or decision about the absurdity, danger, and amorality of the unrealism of innovation, one must first describe the network. (p. 130)

The aim is to use this principle to develop a "symmetric metalanguage" to refer to humans and nonhumans with an "unbiased" vocabulary and adopt it as an analytical stance, not an ethical position (Law, 1992, p. 383).

This opens up to critiques like the claim to adopt an objective stance, and the failure to match the descriptions and explanations that research participants would provide themselves (Murdoch, 2001), questioning the reflexive approach of ANT.

ANT allows moving between different levels of analysis, thus assisting with investigating both the macro- and the microstructures using the same methodological approach. Callon and Latour also supported this viewpoint when they argued that "all differences in level, size, and scope are the result of a battle or a negotiation" (1981, p. 279).

## One Concept, One Technology, and One Metaphor

*Externality, GPS, & Knot*

An externality is a cost or benefit caused by a producer that is not financially incurred or received. An externality (Pigout, 2017) can be positive or negative, and stem from producing or consuming a good or service.

The Global Positioning System (GPS), originally Navstar GPS, is a satellite-based radio navigation system owned by the United States government, and operated by the United States Space Force (https://en.wikipedia.org/wiki/United_States_Space_Force). One of the Global Navigation Satellite Systems

(GNSS) provides geolocation and time information to a GPS receiver anywhere on or near the Earth where there is an unobstructed line of sight to four or more GPS satellites with no obstacles such as mountains and buildings that can block the relatively weak GPS signals.

The GPS provides critical positioning capabilities worldwide to military, civil, and commercial users. The United States government created the system, maintained and controlled it, and made it freely accessible to anyone with a GPS receiver. The GPS does not require the user to transmit any data, and it operates independent of any telephonic or internet reception. However, these technologies can enhance the usefulness of GPS positioning information.

The knot is an interesting metaphor because it is a condensation of links, like the knot of a necklace, a knot in hair, or in a cell phone cord. Also, an identity can have some knots in more extended rhizomes. Deleuze and Guattari (2004) admitted that there are "knots of arborescence in rhizomes and rhizomatic offshoots in roots . . . despotic formations . . . specific to rhizomes, just as there are anarchic deformations in the transcendent system of trees" (p. 93).

Engeström's title book, *From Teams to Knots*, referenced this powerful image. He defined the first principle of "knotworking," meaning the object orientation of an activity. Knots cannot be teams because of their changing memberships and limited time. Moreover, a "negotiated knotworking" (Engeström et al., 2003) expresses the idea of new work practice, where the network of relationships is intertwined to take care, acting toward a finality for a specific aim.

## For Learning Design

The concept of the zone of possibility (ZoP), developed by Cook, Mor, and Santos (2020), builds on the post-Vygotsky perspectives of Daniels (2008). Vygotsky (1978) conceptualized the zone of proximal development as the space where the more knowledgeable other helps a learner, implying an intellectual and power differential of the expert versus the novice.

The ZoP regards learners as having the capacity to inhabit a space of possibility; thus, each learner becomes a zone of socially structured possibility rather than a singular point (Daniels, 2008). In a ZoP, the learners interact in a hybrid social, physical, and digital network to collectively build knowledge. The ZoP allows collective knowledge and contextual learning to emerge dynamically and jointly through equal social positioning.

The zone, the socio-technical system of a hybrid network, provides the space and urges the learners to engage in community practices, thus affording the possibility for learners to benefit from one another. The learner could acquire and find the fertile arrangement to grow and act agentively in this space. Agency plays a central role in the learning process: it becomes a learning objective, helping the learner find a position in and transform the world.

Technology, by itself, does not create forms of engaged learning and promote agency, but the design of specific activities does (Tchounikine, 2019). The focus of the "possible learning zone" means to create and sustain the viable condition to keep the learner, individually and collectively, active, curious, and attentive to the internal and external conditions for the learning.

## TAKEAWAY IDEAS FROM THIS CHAPTER

### Reflecting on Expanding a Teacher Community

In this chapter, we discussed different ways to expand a teacher community. In a teacher community, the ways people grow and exercise leadership to actualize different types of visions are typically complex and require careful analyses from multiple angles. It is important to conduct such analyses because this issue can significantly impact the nature of social interactions, workplace dynamics, and professional development of the professional community members.

Each member of your professional community, including you, could already be exercising different kinds of leadership to expand the teacher community. And this could have been done without clear awareness of how it can influence the nature of the teacher community. For instance, you may not be in an official leadership position, but you could be significantly influencing others and contributing to the expansion of the teacher collective. The same thing may apply to all of the members in your professional community.

An important question is what kinds of leadership need to be exercised to expand your teacher community. Reflecting on this could require you to delve into your value system regarding the nature of the professional community and what underlies this. In a way, this is an existential journey. You will be thinking about who you are and who you want to be in your professional community in relation to your value system. Reflecting on this may not be easy, but your takeaway from it could be quite rewarding and transformational. Again, let us reflect on the following issues by making use of the theoretical frameworks discussed above. Then construct your own takeaways from the chapter by answering the following questions:

- How are those in the leadership positions (i.e., principal, department chairs, etc.) exercising different kinds of leadership and contributing to the

expansion of teacher communities? What do you think are the strengths and weaknesses of their leadership? And if there is room for improvement, what needs to be done?
- In the past, what has been done in your workplace to reflect on and improve the ways those in leadership positions exercise their leadership? How did it work? How do you think it can be improved?
- How do you see the styles of leadership that you and your colleagues are exercising? Does anyone stands out? How do you categorize the type of leadership, and how do you feel about it? And how are the other members of your professional community reacting to the type of leadership?
- Among the different styles of leadership discussed above, which type of leadership do you think you are currently exercising in your professional community? What kind of leadership would you like to exercise? How is it possible in your current position to exercise that type of leadership? If you are already exercising it, in what ways are you doing it for the expansion of your teacher community? If not, what is serving as a barrier? What can be done to overcome this?
- What kind of leadership do you value and why? Is it possible for you to verbalize what kinds of experiences underlie it? How have the experiences affected your value system?
- What are the situations—teacher meetings, lunchroom conversations, lesson study meetings, and so forth—that serve as the arena for you and your professional community members to exercise different types of leadership? What impact has it created, and how has it influenced the teacher community in your workplace? What can be improved?
- What should be done to boost your professional community members' engagement in improving the educational practice? Could it be conceptualized in terms of a certain type of leadership needed in your professional community? If not, what other factors need to be considered? Are there any kinds of physical or online environment needed to improve the situation? What has been done in your workplace and what needs to be done further?

## REFERENCES

Bandura, A. (2003). Cultivate self-efficacy for personal and organizational effectiveness. In E. A. Locke (Ed.), *The Blackwell handbook of principles of organizational behaviour*. Blackwell.

Bass, B. M. (1985). *Leadership and performance beyond expectation*. Free Press.

Brown, G. G. (1995). How do earthworms affect microfloral and faunal community diversity? *Plant and Soil, 170*, 209–231.

Brown, R. (1989). *Group process: Dynamics within and between groups*. Basil Blackwell.

Callon, M., & Latour, B. (1981). Unscrewing the big Leviathan: How actors macro-structure reality and how sociologists help them to do so. In K. D. Knorr-Cetina & A.V. Cocourel (Eds.), *Advances in social theory and methodology: Toward an integration of micro and macro-sociologies* (pp. 277–303). Routledge and Kegan Paul.

Cook, J., Mor, Y., & Santos, P. (2020). Three cases of hybridity in learning spaces: Towards a design for a zone of possibility. *British Journal of Educational Technology, 51*(4), 1155–1167. https://doi.org/10.1111/bjet.12945

Daniels, H. (2008). *Vygotsky and research*. Routledge.

Deleuze, G., & Guattari, F. (2004). *A thousand plateaus: Capitalism and schizophrenia* (B. Massumi, Trans.). Continuum.

Engeström, Y. (1999). Expansive visualization of work: A theoretical activity perspective. *Computer Supported Cooperative Work, 8*, 63–93.

Engeström, Y. (2007). *From teams to knots: Activity-theoretical studies of collaboration and learning at work*. Cambridge University Press.

Engeström, Y., Engeström, R., & Kerosuo, H. (2003). The discursive construction of collaborative care. *Applied Linguistics, 24*(3), 286–315.

Festinger, L. (1957). *A theory of cognitive dissonance*. Stanford University Press.

Hellerman, J. (2021, August 2). *10 screenwriting and directing tips from Chloé Zhao*. No Film School. https://nofilmschool.com/chloe-zhao-screenwriting-tips

Hogg, M. A. (1992). *The social psychology of group cohesiveness*. New York University Press.

House, R. J. (1976). Theory of charismatic leadership. In J. G. Hunt & L. L. Larson (Eds.), *Leadership: The cutting edge* (pp. 189–207). Southern Illinois University Press.

Isaacs, W. N. (1999). *Dialogue and the art of thinking together*. Doubleday.

Johnson, D. W., & Johnson, R. T. (1991). *Cooperation in the classroom*. Interaction.

Latour, B. (1991). Technology is society made durable. In J. Law (Ed.), *A sociology of monsters: Essays on power, technology and domination* (pp. 103–131). Routledge.

Latour, B., Schwartz, C., & Charvolin, F. (1991). Crises des environnements: Défis aux sciences humaines. *Futur Antérieur, 6*, 28–56.

Law, J. (1992). Notes on the theory of the actor-network: Ordering, strategy, and heterogeneity. *Systems Practice, 5*, 379–393.

Levine, J. M., & Moreland, R. L. (1990). Progress in small group research. *Annual Review of Psychology, 41*, 583–634.

Lipnack, J., & Stamps, J. (1997). *Reaching across space, time, and organizations with technology*. Wiley.

Lumsden, G., & Lumsden, D. L. (1996). *Communicating in groups and teams*. Wadsworth.

McMillan, D. W., & Chavis, D. M. (1986). Sense of community: A definition and theory. *Journal of Community Psychology, 14*, 6–23.

Murdoch, J. (2001). Ecologising sociology: Actor-network theory, co-construction and the problem of human exemptionalism. *Sociology, 35*(1), 111–133.

Paskevich, D., Estabrooks, P., Brawley, L., & Carron, A. (2001). *Group cohesion in sport and exercise.* In R. Singer, H. Hausenblas, & C. Janelle (Eds.), *Handbook of sport psychology* (2nd ed., pp. 472–494). Wiley.

Pigou, A. C. (2017). Welfare and economic welfare. In *The economics of welfare* (pp. 3–22). Routledge. doi:10.4324/9781351304368-1

Rost, J. C. (1991). *Leadership for the twenty-first century.* Praeger.

Schachter, S., Ellertson, N., McBride, D., & Gregory, D. (1951). An experimental study of cohesiveness and productivity. *Human Relations, 4*(3), 229–238.

Tajfel, H. (1981). *Human groups and social categories.* Cambridge University Press.

Taylor, D. M., Doria, J. R., & Tyler, J. K. (1983). Group performance and cohesiveness: An attribution analysis. *Journal of Social Psychology, 119,* 187–198.

Tchounikine, P. (2019). Learners' agency and CSCL technologies: Towards an emancipatory perspective. *International Journal of Computer-Supported Collaborative Learning, 14*(2), 237–250. https://10_1007-S11412-019-09302-5

Turner, Victor. (1987). The anthropology of performance. In Victor Turner (Comp.), *The anthropology of performance.* PAJ Publications.

Van Loon, J. (2013). *Risk and technological culture: Towards a sociology of virulence.* Routledge.

Vygotsky, L. (1978). *Mind in society: The development of higher mental processes.* Harvard University Press.

Wenger, E. (1996). Communities of practice: The social fabric of a learning organization. *Healthcare Forum Journal, 39*(4), 20–26.

Wenger, E. (1998). Communities of practice: Learning as a social system. *Systems Thinker, 9*(5), 2–3.

*Chapter Seven*

# Move On

## *The End of a Community*

> Two truths approach each other. One comes from inside, the other from outside, and where they meet we have a chance to catch sight of ourselves.
> —T. Tranströmer (2001)

We arrive at the end of our course in this book: the end of a community. Below, we analyze three main concepts: *exit*, *transformation*, and *disconnection*.

## Exit

After analyzing the processes that hold the group together, we examine the forces that bring instability, questioning the group's survival.

Conflict is always a possible reality in the group. As Levine and Thompson (1996) noted, intergroup conflict can have different outcomes: on the one hand, it can have negative consequences both for individual members and for the entire group; on the other hand, it can have positive results, such as increased creativity in solving problems and unifying proposals.

Conflict within a work group occurs when people who depend on each other have different points of view and different, even conflicting, interests or goals. A good leader is aware that conflict is a natural and potentially productive component in the context of group relationships and interpersonal relationships. Conflict stimulates thought, causes various perspectives about a situation to be considered, and stimulates group members to understand better the critical factors regarding the decision to be made. All this happens when the conflict is well managed consciously and constructively.

The central aspect is not to decide whether to stimulate or avoid conflict but to work it effectively for teamwork. How a conflict within the group is managed can become constructive or destructive. Destructive conflict is present when it interferes with the work's effectiveness and a healthy work climate. Typically, this type of conflict is characterized by competitive communication.

Each group member tries to influence others only to be right about their ideas, solutions, and points of view. This creates a "win-lose" relationship (who wins and who loses). Individual group members believe that only one of them (or a part of them) can "win" and assert themselves over the others, leading them to accept their points of view. These dynamics' rapid deterioration of the group climate and interpersonal relationships are evident.

The presence of the following symptoms can point to destructive conflict: competition between group members; attention to the benefits of the individual; "win-lose" approach (winner-loser) decisions and solutions formulated for the use of only one or a few members of the group; the closed climate in which the group does not accept comments or ideas from people who are not part of the group itself; defensive communication; resistance to change (group members see each new idea or suggestion as a threat to the current way of doing things); and personal attacks. Individuals are ridiculed (or subjected to sarcasm) for expressing their opinions or suggestions.

Constructive conflict is present when the members of a work group know that disagreement is a natural aspect of the group; indeed, it can be a crucial factor in achieving common goals. This type of attitude is reflected in how communicating is characterized by cooperation: listening to the ideas and opinions of others with attention, interest, and positivity. Communication is used to highlight the common objectives of the group members and the factors that unite them. It is a type of communication that encourages a "win-win" orientation, in which everyone can claim to be a winner.

Communication should highlight the interest of the group members in listening to each other's ideas and points of view, the willingness to change their perspective on an issue, and respect for the integrity of other group members and the opinions they represent to encourage constructive conflict. This leads people to freely express and motivate their points of view, focusing on the content of the themes rather than on character or character aspects. In this context, people feel at ease expressing their thoughts and actively and constructively participating in group activities.

For these reasons, constructive conflict is an essential factor in the effectiveness of teamwork. Indeed, it allows group members to broaden their understanding of the issues involved, enabling them to develop a broader range of ideas and solutions. The mechanisms that groups use to deal with conflict are:

- *Conflict avoidance*: this is aimed at preventing the appearance of conflict.
- *Conflict reduction*: intervention aimed at reducing or eliminating a conflict that has already started and has become relevant for the group.
- *Conflict creation*: intentional production or exacerbation of the conflict.

Conflicts are often latent, and group members are unaware of them (Deutsch, 1973).

The deviant is the one who presents positions that are different from those of the majority, therefore considered to perturb the cohesion and uniformity of the group. The deviant is perceived by the group as a threat to the cohesion and uniformity of the group. To bring members back into the "reassuring" ranks of the majority, the group can increase the number of communications and persuasive acts. If this strategy fails, the deviant can be kicked out of the group or reduced to a harmless condition because he is marginalized.

These dynamics were studied by Schachter, who conducted a famous 1951 experiment on intragroup deviance to learn how the deviant was treated in the group. The in-group variables for studying the phenomena relating to the acceptance or rejection of the deviant are:

- *The deviant* is the person who waits for a slightly more majority position to emerge in the group, with the obligation to support the opposite opinion until the end of the discussion.
- *The slider* is the one who slips, who changes his opinion, and aligns himself with what the group decides during the discussion.
- *The mode* supports opinions that are primarily in the majority.

Another possible expression of dissent is the position of the minority—Serge Moscovici (1984) placed minority innovation at the center of the scientific debate. Moscovici criticizes seeing the social system as something already preestablished. The conflicts between the members are minimal, and all who reject the norms are excluded because they are seen as deviant. The author elaborated on the genetic model of social influence, where all group members are carriers and receivers of social impact.

The minorities in question are "active" or "nomic" minorities, that is, made up of one or more people who become aware of having been segregated as a minority due to specific characteristics or conduct, based on which they structure strong convictions capable of producing particular rules of conduct, consensual points of view, coherent purposes. The size of the minority depends mainly on the style of behavior and negotiation it adopts.

A decisive role for the minority to influence the majority is the style of behavior: it must be consistent (i.e., it must maintain its decisions with a diachronic consistency over time) with a synchronic consistency (all who are part of the minority group hold the same thesis with a stable consensus); be autonomous (i.e., concerning external ties) and flexible (i.e., capable of negotiating to maintain consistency); be equitable (or look at other positions with impartiality); and involve investment and demonstrate involvement.

Minority dissent promotes divergent (i.e., creative) thinking, which stimulates individuals and groups to consider the problem posed by the minority from multiple perspectives and produce original solutions. In contrast, the majority does convergent thinking. It becomes a priority to adhere to the shared norm, fossilizing the group on a single position and blocking the search process for possible alternatives.

Generally, the deviant leaves the group to safeguard her identity, or she stays inside and accepts the majority position. This could be done through the use of different strategies:

- *Ridicule*: it is a strategy that tends to show deviants as somewhat pathetic characters, obsessed with which it is possible to joke, make jokes, and laugh. The sanction of social ridicule is powerful enough to reduce the strength of these people (e.g., the painting movement of the Impressionists had been ridiculed by the artistic establishment of the time that saw this pictorial current as a threat).
- *Naturalization*: it is a form of resistance to take away the credibility of the deviant.
- *Biologization*: it consists in attributing essential, biological characteristics to the deviant, for which he cannot be believed (sex, race, a handicap).
- *Psychologization*: consists of applying a psychological label to the deviant: she is paranoid, neurotic, too anxious, so she is given a brand name that aims to neutralize her credibility.
- *Socialization*: refers to the characteristics of social belonging of the subject.

The possible reactions of the majority to the innovations are:

- *Explicit and partial refusal*: in this case, the deviant is not accepted; he is considered an impostor, and natural or symbolic expulsion from the group can occur.
- *Partial refusal*: if the majority of the group realizes that the deviant is not all wrong, she also says the right things. Still, the deviant is not popular because she could compromise the group's reputation.
- *Disconfirmation*: through silence, the seemingly indifferent minority position is accepted. This strategy denies the role of the deviant, nullifying his identity.

This transaction often also involves changing how we see ourselves, restructuring the unique structure, and putting social belonging and even social identity into play. For this reason, according to Berger and Luckmann (1966), one can speak of betrayal toward the former group and parts of one's self.

The passage toward the exit of the group, as well as the entrance, can be characterized by ceremonial rites that mark its symbolic value. The value attributed to leaving the group is conditioned by how salient the group's membership was, understood by Moscovici and Doise (1991) as a high level of participation and exchange with the other group members. Another critical element was achieving a common goal, giving rise to a significant affective tone (which can be positive and negative), affecting the productivity and satisfaction of the members. The more these dimensions mark the membership, the more the exit from the group will be experienced as a significant loss, such as becoming an event to be celebrated in one's biography.

Regarding the exit transaction, Tajfel's (1981) social behavior moves along a continuum, never touching extremes but placing themselves in intermediate areas that go in the direction of both extremes. The essential condition for the emergence of interpersonal or intergroup behaviors is also the beliefs of reference of individuals: when the individual believes he is in "social mobility" and passes from one group to another, he considers the boundaries permeable, looking for who satisfies his own social image; on the contrary, if the individual believes that the boundaries between groups are well defined and not flexible, it becomes difficult to pass from one group to another.

**Transformation**

For Wenger (2011), participation in a community of practice creates continuity and discontinuity between those who participated and those who did not participate. These discontinuities are noted in the moments of crossing, in which "the transition from one community of practice to another can lead to a real transformation" (Wenger, 1998, p. 121).

Wenger (2011) introduced two types of connection between communities: intermediary factors and boundary objects. Borders become an object of interest under their duality of relationship toward the inside of their community and toward the outside. In particular, the concept of border crossing outlines how the two systems meet and "contaminate."

The first term refers to people who engage in brokering practices capable of introducing course elements into other communities. In crossing borders, mediators play a vital role because they can propose new features from one community of practice to another. For example, students introduced to an internship can be considered "mediators" as they bring new tools and insights between the school/university world and the business world.

Border meetings are significant for transforming and enriching practices, which can respond to different purposes. Wenger (2011) identified different levels of the border: the face-to-face conversation between two members allows both to be transparent but not very influential in the rest of the process; visiting a practice offers broader exposure to the community of practice, and how members engage with each other while remaining one way (knowledge flows only to one of the two communities involved).

Finally, extended participation in the time forces a greater immersion in each other's practices, leading to a more intense and participatory exchange. The practice can turn into a connection in three ways:

1. *Border practices*: If a border meeting, whether formal like a task force or informal like lunch break conversations, becomes habitual and constitutes a constant space of mutual engagement, a new practice is likely to emerge. It is configured as a form of collective intermediation that runs the risk of becoming a community of practice in its own right.
2. *Overlap*: does not require a specific border company but is provided by a direct and lasting overlap between two practices.
3. *Suburbs*: intended as a partially internal and partially external area of change. It consists of connecting with other people who are not destined to become full practice members. In this way, nonbinding and informal ways of access are offered (such as observation) without suffering the pressures of full membership. The periphery transmits a specific permeability and dynamism around the practice, with different levels of involvement of outsiders and offering multiple and diversified learning opportunities.

On the one hand, Wenger (2011) pointed out the difference between border and periphery, which represent the "limits" of communities of practice and points of contact with the world: borders evoke discontinuities, lines of separation between the inside and the outside, belonging and nonbelonging, inclusion and exclusion.

On the other hand, peripherality is an ambiguous condition that can jealously guard information or make it available and accessible. Both are closely intertwined and necessary, putting the CoP in a situation of osmosis with the outside world.

The concept of boundary is also the subject of reflection in the theory of activity, designating two activity systems that merge and generate a third familiar and new object. Engeström (2003) identified the "boundary zone" intended as a border area or, rather, as a physical and symbolic place where the interaction occurs. This perspective refers to the need to consider the dialogic dimension (Bakhtin, 1982) between different systems, which meet and contaminate each other.

## Disconnection

The actor-network theory (ANT) considers the production of meaning as an activity of connecting/disconnecting and analyzing how actors come to be created through collaborations of other actors in different contexts. The different actors' perspectives create the explicit links on which we can reconstruct implicit meaning: the ties precede the nodes (Mutzel, 2009, p. 878).

It means that the connections are central. If the ties are disconnected, the structure becomes weak and is destroyed. Collective actor networks are made of flesh and fabric, words and memories, contracts and laws, money and transactions, and, increasingly, cables and protocols. The tangible side of the networks brings materiality to the social dimensions, quickly changing like a "Prometheus" form.

The three perspectives above show how the community is destined for transformation. The end and dissolution of the community are anticipated by the temporal sessions and the activity planned for a final assessment.

Moreover, habits, like daily or weekly communication, have to change. What is often missing in teacher community-oriented professional learning and development is a true reflection of the way and opportunities to sustain practices over time. Bridging the gap between formative experiences and professional practices is the hidden task before the conclusion. So, understanding how the new competencies or the new learning are sustained provides valuable information about their future influence on professional development.

Teachers could introduce new practices in significantly different ways, often grafting new approaches on top of existing practices without altering classroom routines. A significant change is necessary, altering instruction, beliefs about teaching and learning, and pedagogical practice. The mentor and the trainer are responsible for starting the reflexive process of sustainability in the learners to capitalize on the work.

## One Concept, One Technology, and One Metaphor

*Diffractive Learning, Digital Application, and Grafting*

Below are three concepts that express a form of fragmentation of information and relationships, which quickly leads to a situation of precariousness, instability, and a new possible outcome from the action.

The diffractive pedagogies pay attention to the inseparability between the knower and the known, the teacher and the taught, and learning/teaching bodies and the pedagogical environments and apparatus involved (Hickey-Moody et al., 2016). The material embodied and affective nature of teaching and learning are mutually implicated. Disciplinary boundaries are traversed for an open, unpredictable, performative learning experience not yet present in any preexisting structure.

The fragmentary perspective of the diffractive methodology applied to the learning process can be linked to the continued use of social networks and digital applications in our smartphones. In information and communication technology, a *mobile application* (also known by the abbreviation app, from the English mobile application, or mobile app) is a software application dedicated to mobile devices, such as smartphones or tablets, typically designed and implemented in a lighter format in terms of hardware resources used.

The dance of connecting and disconnecting is evident in the use of the applications: the need to go out from the applications shows an attempt to retake control of time and attention instead of a continuous scrolling. Digital detox has gained popularity as a period when a person voluntarily refrains from using digital devices such as smartphones, computers, and social media platforms.

Using an agricultural metaphor, the image that we propose is that of grafting. Grafting or graftage is a horticultural technique whereby tissues are joined to continue their growth. The success of this joining requires that the vascular tissues grow together, and such joining is called inosculation. The upper part of the combined plant is called the scion (/ˈsaɪən/), while the lower part is called the rootstock. The technique is most commonly used in the asexual propagation of commercially grown plants for horticultural and agricultural trades.

Usually, one plant is selected for its roots; this plant is called the stock or rootstock. The other plant is selected for its stems, leaves, flowers, or fruits, and it is called the scion or cion. The scion contains the desired genes to be duplicated in future production by the stock/scion plant. In stem grafting, a standard method, a shoot of a selected, desired plant cultivar is grafted onto the stock of another type. In another common form called bud grafting, a dormant side bud is grafted onto the stem of another stock plant.

When it has inosculated successfully, the plant is encouraged to grow by pruning off the stem of the stock plant just above the newly grafted bud. For successful grafting to take place, the vascular cambium tissues of the stock and scion plants must be placed in contact with each other. Both tissues must be kept alive until the graft has "taken," usually after a few weeks. Successful grafting only requires a vascular connection between the grafted tissues.

The diffractive dimension, the continuous and intermittent use of digital applications, and the grafting activity are in progress: the outcome of the activity is uncertain, new, and unpredictable. These three concepts can help to think of the community that ends as a practice in renewal, that closes as a cycle, and that can reopen in a new and different form.

## For Learning Design

### Affectivity Scaffolding

The notion of affective scaffolding is defined by Candiotto and Dreon (2021):

> affective scaffolding is a unique hermeneutical tool that plays a fundamental role in drawing attention to the continuous and recursive interactions with the environment shaping affectivity. (p. 3)

The reflection started with Griffiths and Scarantino's (2005), in the paper "Emotions in the Wild," understanding of emotions as both social and intersubjective phenomena. It is proposed as an example of "situated affectivity": the environment influences and is influenced by the unfolding of emotions, constantly reframing the relationships and offering action possibilities in the form of emotions.

The social embeddedness of emotions is both synchronous (supporting an emotional episode) and diachronic (supporting the development of a repertoire of emotional abilities). Affective scaffolding refers to those resources that contribute to affective regulation if integrated into structured and repeated interaction practices.

Krueger (2015) proposed three distinctions:

1. *Embodied affective scaffoldings*, in which the affective experience is regulated by a range of physical processes distributed throughout our bodies, such as digestion.
2. *Social affective scaffoldings*, in which socially distributed feedback loops regulate the affective dynamics of individuals and groups, such as family dinners.
3. *Material affective scaffoldings*, in which affectivity is regulated by the material culture that comprises particular objects and environments, such as a wedding dress.

Recently, Candiotto and Dreon (2021) stressed the habits in affective scaffolding to shape the interactions. Affective scaffolding could be adopted in the learning design as a tentative way to release tensions, fear, and regulation of emotions in the learning, like overwhelming feelings relating to the task to fulfill, the code of communication to sustain, and the role to perform.

To apply this process at the end of the community, which is a relatively sensible moment, before closing the activity and often the social relationship developed, the teacher could introduce the specific activity to open a safe space for sharing emotions.

Some examples to apply are related to the broad area of social-emotional learning (SEL) activities (art activities, self-awareness activities, mindfulness activities, goal-setting activities) or concrete step-by-step activity as the WOOP exercise (described at https://characterlab.org/activities/woop-for-classrooms). It proposes different steps, starting by identifying a wish or goal you want to achieve; next, you mentally imagine one positive outcome of achieving this goal and one obstacle that stands in the way; finish with a plan for how you can get around that obstacle.

A literacy of sensitivity is what can be created by participating in a group, community, and network and what can also be mediated by technology.

## TAKEAWAY IDEAS FROM THIS CHAPTER

### Reflecting on Conflicts and Transformations

In this chapter, we discussed key theoretical frameworks to make sense of conflicts in a professional community. You might have experienced—or are currently experiencing—different forms of conflict in your workplace. Conflicts may not be resolved quickly, and if they are sustained, they can bring people into a gridlock situation. It can be quite frustrating for anyone who is involved in a conflict situation, and this can lead people to psychologically disconnect themselves from the professional community—or in the worst-case scenario, exit from the profession. Depending on how conflicts take place or are resolved, your experience in the teacher community could be totally different.

In your workplace, there must have been attempts to avoid and overcome different kinds of conflicts. But what is difficult about a conflict is that people develop their own interpretations of the situation, and these interpretations can be different from one another. This discrepancy in interpretation is often unavoidable and can be a key source of conflict. Once it takes place, a conflict can be devastating and may set a negative tone of your experiences in your profession.

But it is also true that a conflict can offer an opportunity for professional growth. For instance, suppose that, in a teacher meeting, you proposed an idea to use part of the school budget for updating information and communication technology for teaching, but other teachers maintained that such use of the budget would be worthless. After a number of meetings, no consensus was built, and the gridlock seemed to be the only outcome. In such a situation, you could make efforts to view the situation from multiple angles and develop a creative solution to overcome the gridlock. Through such efforts, you may engage in sincere dialogues with the people on the other side and consider perspectives that you have not considered before. Such experiences could have helped you to learn the importance of communicating with diverse community members and put yourself in their shoes. You could have also learned that merely proposing what you think is right does not necessarily solve the situation; that you need to see the big picture and be in touch with the perceptions of diverse people in your professional community to propose creative solutions.

As noted above, you might have had similar experiences and learned how to overcome different types of conflicts. This is a very important kind of learning and transformation as a professional. Using the questions below, reflect on your experiences of this issue based on the theoretical frameworks discussed above and create your own takeaways from the chapter. Here are some guiding questions:

- What kind of conflicts have you experienced in your professional community? Who was involved, and why did the conflict happen? What happened after that?
- What attitude and role do you typically take when a conflict emerges in your professional community? Why do you take this attitude and role? What experiences and value systems seem to underlie there?
- Do conflicts in your workplace emerge due to differences in perspective between majority and minority groups? If so, where does the difference stem from? What can be done to bridge and overcome the differences in perspective?
- Was there any colleague who left your professional community because of conflicts that took place in your professional community? How did your professional community respond to the departure of the colleague? What is your interpretation of the incident? How do you think your professional community should have responded? What can be done to avoid something similar from happening in the future?
- In conflicts, do any persons serve as mediators in your workplace? How has the mediation worked, and why? Suppose that you disagreed with your colleague's opinion about a textbook choice, and you went through lengthy discussions that seemed to go nowhere. Then a mediator came in and introduced a creative idea to use a supplementary textbook that works for both sides. Do you remember such experiences where your colleague served as a mediator? How did the mediator communicate with both sides and make a contribution to overcome the conflict?

- Have you had a mentor who supported you to go through and overcome conflicts? How has the mentorship worked? What can be done to institutionalize such a mentorship as a system in your professional community?
- How do you see your own contributions to mediate others to overcome conflicts in your professional community? What is your approach to mediate conflicts or mentor those who are caught in conflicts? How do you think such experiences could contribute to the growth and development of your community members—and you?
- How do you feel about the possibility that external agents, experts, or consultants play a role in mediating conflicts in your workplace? Have you had any experience of having others outside your institution mediate conflicts? If so, how useful was it? If not, why not?
- How do you think conflicts shape your professional identity and the nature of teacher communities in your workplace? How important do you think is the experience to explore creative solutions to overcome conflicts as a professional? What is your experience of this? What did you learn from the experience?

## REFERENCES

Bakhtin, M. M. (1982). *The dialogic imagination by M. M. Bakhtin: Four essays* (Caryl Emerson, Trans.). University of Texas Press.

Berger, P. L., & Luckmann, T. (1966). *The social construction of reality*. Doubleday.

Candiotto, L., & Dreon, R. (2021). Affective scaffoldings as habits: A pragmatist approach. *Frontiers in Psychology, 12*, 945. https://doi.org/10.3389/fpsyg.2021.629046

Deutsch, M. (1973). *The resolution of conflict: Constructive and destructive processes*. Yale University Press.

Engeström, Y. (2003). The horizontal dimension of expansive learning: Weaving a texture of cognitive trails in the terrain of health care in Helsinki. *Milestones of Vocational and Occupational Education and Training, 1*, 152–179.

Griffiths, P. E., & Scarantino, A. (2005). Emotions in the wild: The situated perspective on emotion. In *The Cambridge handbook of situated cognition*. Cambridge University Press.

Hickey-Moody, A., Palmer, H., & Sayers, E. (2016). Diffractive pedagogies: Dancing across new materialist imaginaries. *Gender and Education, 28*(2), 213–229.

Krueger, J. (2015). The affective "we": Self-regulation and shared emotions. In *Phenomenology of sociality* (pp. 263–278). Routledge.

Levine, J. M., & Thompson, L. (1996). Conflict in groups. In E. T. Higgins & A. Kruglanski (Eds.), *Social psychology: Handbook of basic principles* (pp. 745–776). Guilford.

Moscovici, S. (1984). *Psicología social*. Anthropos Editorial.

Moscovici, S., & Doise, W. (1991). *Dissensions et consensus. Une théorie genérale des décisions collectives.* Presses Universitaires de France.

Mutzel, S. (2009). Networks as culturally constituted processes: A comparison of relational sociology and actor-network theory. *Current Sociology, 57*(2009), 871–887. doi:10.1177/0011392109342223

Schachter, S. (1951). Deviation, rejection, and communication. *Journal of Abnormal and Social Psychology, 46*, 190–208.

Tajfel, H. (1981). *Human groups and social categories.* Cambridge University Press.

Tranströmer, T. (2001). *The half-finished heaven: The best poems of Tomas Tranströmer* (Robert Bly, Trans.). Graywolf Press.

Wenger, E. (1998). *Communities of practice: Learning, meaning and identity.* Cambridge University Press.

Wenger, E. (2011). *Communities of practice: A brief introduction.* University of Oregon Scholars' Bank. https://scholarsbank.uoregon.edu/xmlui/bitstream/handle/1794/11736/A%20brief%20introduction%20to%20CoP.pdf?sequence=1&isAllowed=y

*Part II*

*Chapter Eight*

# Teacher Education in the Global South and Open-Source Hardware

Amit Dhakulkar and Karen Ferreira-Meyers

## INTRODUCTION

Teacher training has been a thorny issue in the Global South for many decades. Open education is seeking to address some of the teacher training aspects that await urgent solutions. In their chapter on teacher education and open science principles, Ferreira-Meyers and Dhakulkar (2021) proposed a model based on open-science principles through which important elements of defective teacher training could be addressed.

Parts of this model are easier to implement than others (e.g., communities of practice already exist and can, fairly easily, be developed or even set up from the grassroots level). One of the aspects that might not be that easy to solve is the hardware, which is part of how teachers, learners, and other key education stakeholders link, interact, share, and grow.

In this chapter, we look at open-source hardware (OSH, also known as open hardware) and propose ways of integrating it in teacher education to address some of the previously identified challenges in this field. To do so, we detail some problematic areas of teacher education in the Global South before proposing some definitions and examples of open hardware. This goes hand in hand with the notion of community of practice (CoP), which we situate in a framework we designed in 2021 (Ferreira-Meyers & Dhakulkar, 2021).

A survey of existing literature brings us to selected recommendations regarding the use of open hardware in teacher training as well as in the area of teaching and learning of science, in particular, and, more generally, in a variety of school and university subjects.

## Challenges to Teacher Education

So, what issues do we encounter as teacher educators and teachers? How well are we able to implement what we learn in pre- and in-service environments? When we look at existing research in the field, we notice several problem areas. They include, among others, the fact that we often work in isolation and do not share some of the innovative ideas we implement locally, in our schools, or even just in a particular classroom. One way of dealing with it is to set up communities of practice (CoPs)—we discuss this a bit further in this chapter—so that we have a dynamic platform for sharing new approaches and methods, but also for learning from each other.

Another key aspect where we, as teachers and teacher educators, sometimes feel restricted is resources (financial, human, but also technical and technological) and technology. Researchers have expressed concerns about the increasing costs of equipment necessary to do state-of-the-art scientific research, coupled with the decreasing amount of funding available to be shared between an ever-growing number of labs and researchers. This is particularly so in the Global South.

Technological resources suffer from similar problems. Technology, we know, has two major components: software and hardware. Open software probably is something we have heard of more frequently than open hardware. This is why, in this chapter, we want to look at open hardware and how this can assist us to do our job more efficiently and effectively.

A brief literature review shows some of the following issues experienced in teacher training or teacher education. Several studies focus on science teacher education in the African context. For example, De Beer (2016) described the fact that there are insufficient well-qualified science and mathematics teachers in our schools as the first major challenge, in the particular context of South Africa.

The second challenge he highlighted is an examination-driven school system that lacks focus on affective outcomes of our schooling system. The third one—of essence in this chapter—is that many schools lack appropriate equipment and materials for effective teaching and learning (p. 34).

Earlier on, Le Grange (2007) noted the neglect of indigenous knowledge systems (IKS), which brings about a gap between the learners' everyday experiences and contexts, their sociocultural background (De Beer, 2019a), and what they learn (or are supposed to learn) in schools and universities.

What is being proposed in our educational institutions from a mainly (and often exclusively) Western perspective presents a decontextualized view and alienates the learners. Since the identification of the importance of IKS, there has been a sustained effort to "decolonize" the curriculum and produce coherent approaches that combine the two views (e.g., see De Beer [2019b] and Le Grange [2016]).

Given this background, in addition to the curricula and the classroom practices that have been developed in European contexts, software and hardware that come from the same Western origin will not work as expected in the contexts of the Global South.

As also identified in Ferreira-Meyers and Dhakulkar (2021), another reason for the mismatch stems from the dominant use of European languages (English in particular) in academia and in teacher training. This has had an important consequence; namely, local languages are less valued, less used, and thus less "thought" in to find solutions that work for the Global South. Hall and Tandon (2017) and Santos (2015) are among researchers who speak of epistemicide in this case—the killing of knowledge systems.

While work on open educational resources (OER) has been trying to counter the lack of quality teaching–learning resources, little has been done when it comes to open hardware. Our point of departure is the use of open science principles for the benefit of enhanced teacher education, and, ultimately, improved education in the Global South. Below is an image that shows the links between the various components of open science. This will then allow us to discuss a bit more in detail what open hardware is all about.

Figure 8.1 shows how open hardware is one of the components of open science, in addition to other important elements that have a bearing on teacher education, such as open software, open data, open educational resources, to name but a few.

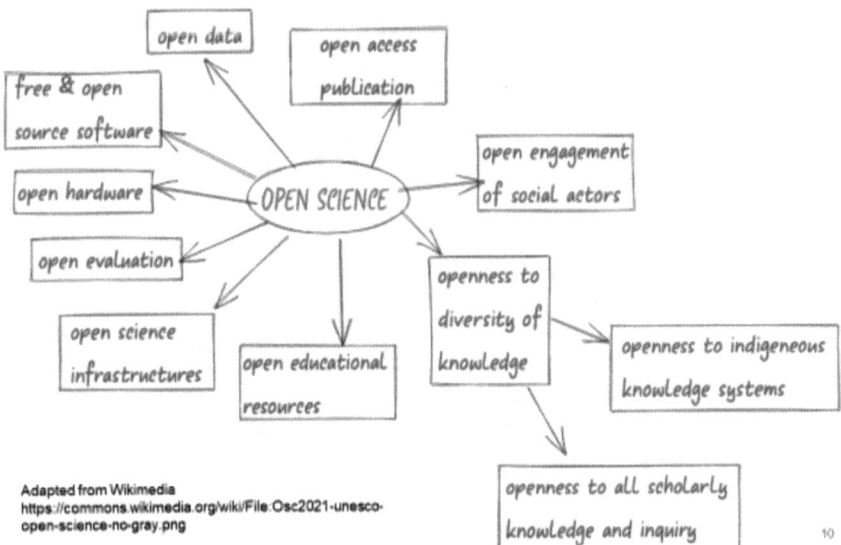

**Figure 8.1. Open Science**
*Source:* Wikimedia

## What Is Open Hardware?

We will start with the question, what is "open"? In the past decade, the term "open" has become fairly well known in the context of various open initiatives such as open educational resources (OERs), open access (OA), free and open-source software (FOSS), among many others.

The core idea in all of the open initiatives is the idea of anyone being able to use content due to licensing conditions. The copyright licenses, which are otherwise very restrictive of the usage by anyone, are in turn used to give users freedom to use the artifact. Among the most commonly known open licenses are the creative commons (CC) licenses (https://creativecommons.org/). For example, the content on Wikipedia is released with a CC BY Share Alike license. This inversion of granting users rights to use instead of restricting them is sometimes known, by a clever play on words, as *copyleft*. So with this little background regarding the idea of open we come to the question of what open hardware is.

Let us look at some of the definitions of open hardware—also known as open-source hardware (OSH) and free and open-source hardware (FOSH). We will use the term open hardware (OH) in this chapter:

> Open source hardware is hardware whose design is made publicly available so that anyone can study, modify, distribute, make, and sell the design or hardware based on that design. The hardware's source, the design from which it is made, is available in the preferred format for making modifications to it.
>
> Ideally, open source hardware uses readily-available components and materials, standard processes, open infrastructure, unrestricted content, and open-source design tools to maximize the ability of individuals to make and use hardware. Open-source hardware gives people the freedom to control their technology while sharing knowledge and encouraging commerce through the open exchange of designs. (https://freedomdefined.org/OSHW)

"Open hardware," or "open-source hardware," refers to the design specifications of a physical object that are licensed in such a way that the object can be studied, modified, created, and distributed by anyone. Open hardware is a set of design principles and legal practices, not a specific type of object. The term can therefore refer to any number of objects—such as automobiles, chairs, computers, robots, or even houses.

Open hardware's source code should be readily accessible, and its components preferably are easy for anyone to obtain. Essentially, open hardware eliminates common roadblocks to the design and manufacture of physical goods; it provides as many people as possible the ability to construct, remix, and share their knowledge of hardware design and function (https://opensource.com/resources/what-open-hardware).

All of these definitions have the following in common: shared design, licensing, design aspects, protocols, and control software. Let us look at each of these in a bit more detail.

*Shared design*: OH includes sharing of design of the hardware, which includes design specifications, printed circuit board (PCB) schematics, blueprints, logic design, and hardware description language (HDL) source. This makes it possible for the users to understand the design of the OH artifact and make it available in the preferred formats.

The design tools used for creating the designs are also free and open-source software, so that users need not have specialized proprietary software to read and work with the design files.

*Licensing* (legal practice): The licensing is such that anyone can study, modify, distribute, make, remix, and sell the design. This is closely related to the four freedoms of free software, and the 5Rs of OERs, and users get this right from the license under which the OH is released. The four freedoms of free software are:

1. The freedom to run the program as you wish, for any purpose (freedom 1).
2. The freedom to study how the program works and to change it so it does your computing as you wish (freedom 2). Access to the source code is a precondition for this.
3. The freedom to redistribute copies so you can help your neighbor (freedom 3).
4. The freedom to distribute copies of your modified versions to others (freedom 4). By doing this you can give the whole community a chance to benefit from your changes. Access to the source code is a precondition (https://www.gnu.org/philosophy/free-sw.html.en).

Similarly, the 5Rs of OERs define what can be done with OERs:

1. *Retain*: the right to make, own, and control copies of the content (e.g., download, duplicate, store, and manage)
2. *Reuse*: the right to use the content in a wide range of ways (e.g., in a class, in a study group, on a website, in a video)
3. *Revise*: the right to adapt, adjust, modify, or alter the content itself (e.g., translate the content into another language)
4. *Remix*: the right to combine the original or revised content with other open content to create something new (e.g., incorporate the content into a mashup)
5. *Redistribute*: the right to share copies of the original content, your revisions, or your remixes with others (e.g., give a copy of the content to a friend) (https://lumenlearning.zendesk.com/hc/en-us/articles/219255947-The-5Rs-of-OER).

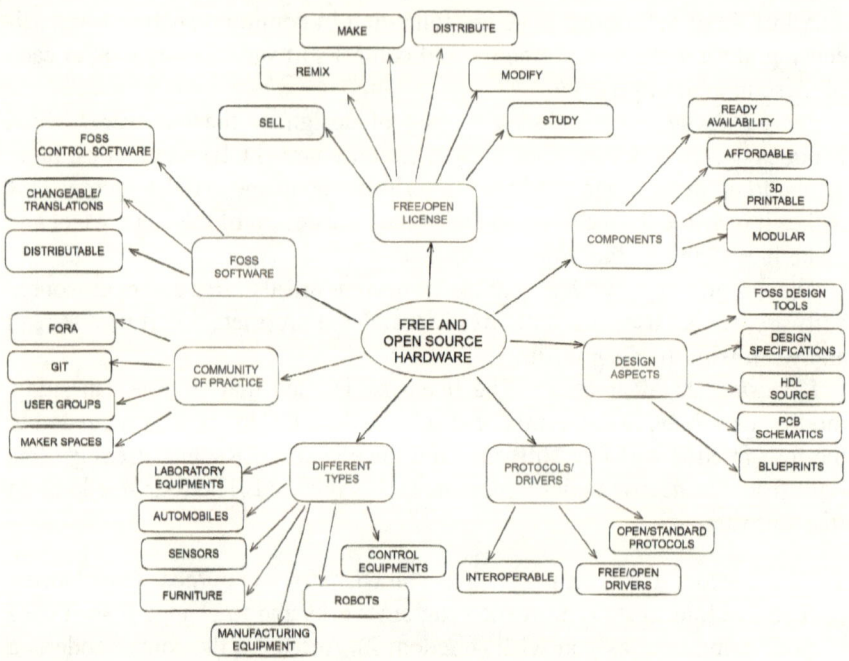

**Figure 8.2. Different Aspects of Free and Open Source Hardware**
*Source:* Wikipedia

*Design aspects*: Usually the parts and materials used in OH have ready availability or can be 3-D-printed by the users. In some cases, the design is modular.

*Protocols*: The various protocols that are used are standard and open protocols so that the data obtained can be used without any issue. The use of open protocol also enables interoperability among different devices and software.

*Control software*: The software used to control the hardware is also released under free and open-source license. This enables the users to modify and translate the software to meet their needs.

The visual above (created by Amit Dhakulkar for this publication) gives an overview of the components and possible interactions of these components of open hardware.

With this introduction to the idea of open hardware, we now look at how this idea can be integrated with and leveraged in teaching and learning.

## Open-Hardware Approach to Teaching and Learning

In their overview of publications on the use of open-source hardware in education, Heradio et al. (2018) identified two educational motivations for using open hardware: First, open hardware has the potential to improve teaching methods as it provides students with experimentation resources that help them to understand abstract concepts of science and engineering. Second, it has the potential to reduce costs as open technologies are often cheaper than their corresponding proprietary alternatives. The authors note that because

> the designs of OSWH devices are freely shared they can be reused at no expense. As experimentation is essential to learn engineering and scientific disciplines, and OSWH can diminish laboratory costs, multiple publications discuss the positive impact that OSWH can have, for instance, in the context of undeveloped countries where labs have been practically unaffordable to date, or to create innovative laboratories. (p. 72099)

A third justification for using open hardware in education is that it has the potential to promote students' engagement because it is appealing and fostering student creativity. For the purpose of improved teaching, open hardware applications can assist in collecting learning analytics by, for example, geolocating the place where students are or accounting for the time students work together.

The idea of open hardware aligns well with the idea of open educational practices (OEPs) as the learners and teachers can have a lot of autonomy in designing interventions. This is primarily because of the openness of the processes and products.

## Communities of Practice (CoP) and Open Hardware

The variety of open movements survive and sustain because of vibrant community participation. As such, open hardware is no exception. This idea of participatory community is described as community of practice (CoP). In brief (and as discussed at length in a preceding chapter), a CoP is a group of people who share a common concern, a set of problems, or an interest in a topic and who come together to fulfill both individual and group goals (Wenger, 2011).

When it comes to teacher education, several CoPs could be in existence, one among teachers, one among students, and even one among teachers and students. As "systems of collective critical inquiry and reflection focused on building . . . collective intelligence" (www.connectededucators.org), these CoPs present themselves in four different types:

1. *Helping Communities* (provide a forum for community members to help each other with everyday work needs).
2. *Best Practice Communities* (develop and disseminate best practices, guidelines, and strategies for their members' use).

3. *Knowledge Stewarding Communities* (organize, manage, and steward a body of knowledge from which community members can draw).
4. *Innovation Communities* (create breakthrough ideas, new knowledge, and new practices).

One reason open hardware has been possible is due to community participation. In this particular case, by community we refer to the developers and designers of open hardware and their users. The making and subsequent improvement of open hardware is essentially a community activity, as can be seen in the various GIT repositories, fora, and user groups. (GIT is a version control system for any type of code or documentation. GIT also allows other users to contribute to a project and report bugs. Several implementations of GIT exist, the most popular being http://github.com and http://gitlab.com.)

Another very important aspect of CoP in the context of open hardware are maker spaces. Maker spaces are places accessible to anyone (sometimes with a fee) to use the expertise and equipment. Maker spaces and open hardware have developed together over the past decade or so. Maker spaces often provide a physical implementation for designing and making open hardware artifacts. Several maker spaces have been implemented in schools. Maker spaces as learning spaces have been suggested by different educational researchers for some time. Implementations have run at different scales. In India, a national-level program known as Atal Tinkering Labs (https://aim.gov.in/atl.php) has been implemented in more than ten thousand schools and caters to more than 7.5 million learners.

One of the ways of implementing open hardware in the context of schools and colleges would be creating maker spaces accessible to learners and integrated with their syllabus. Maker spaces empower learners to learn by doing, tinkering, exploring, and sharing their skills and knowledge with peers. In maker spaces, a do-it-yourself culture is implemented. It also can be seen as a CoP embedded in physical space with necessary tools, equipment, and materials. According to Martinez and Stager (2019),

> makerspaces are places where participants may work together to create and co-create knowledge and physical or digital products. A making environment provides the potential for cross-curricular connections, collaboration, creativity, innovation, and learning.

Maker spaces are constructionist learning spaces, which allow ownership of learning and allow for *tinkering*. The concept of tinkering comes from Seymour Papert's constructionist pedagogy. Tinkering can be understood as an "approach [which] is characterized by a playful, experimental, iterative style of engagement, in which makers are continually reassessing their goals, exploring new paths, and imagining new possibilities" (Resnick & Rosenbaum, 2013, p. 164). This approach toward learning can be best actualized in a maker space. Maker spaces have all the components needed for tinkering.

Maker spaces in schools can be an excellent way to set up CoPs and to implement open educational practices. Several studies now focus on the use of maker spaces as learning contexts. Mersand (2021; Mersand et al., 2018) provides an overview of research related to maker spaces. For example, Eriksson et al. (2018) look at implementation of maker spaces in schools; Keune and Peppler (2019) elaborate on the various materials that can be used in maker spaces. Paganelli et al. (2017) discuss maker spaces in the context of teacher professional development and note that

> if we want teachers to implement the type of best practices highlighted as effective in research, it is imperative that teachers are having the same type of experiences when participating in professional development. (p. 234)

Agreeing with this point, we note that maker spaces and experience in establishing and working in them constitute excellent opportunities for teachers to get acquainted with practical, hands-on knowledge required to use open hardware in their own teaching and learning contexts. We cannot expect teachers to effectively use open hardware and OEPs if they are not confident about using them or tinkering with them or have doubts regarding their applicability.

## Examples of OH Applications in the Real World

A comprehensive list of open hardware/FOSH projects can be found on Wikipedia (https://en.wikipedia.org/wiki/List_of_open-source_hardware_projects). We describe some of the most common projects that have found uses in education, particularly at the high school and college levels. In addition to what is detailed below, useful literature on open hardware in education can be found at https://rheradio.github.io/OSHWInEducation/.

Another interesting case is that of Safecast, a participatory, citizen-science centered, open-source radiation mapping initiative, which developed open-source radiation monitors in the aftermath of the Fukushima Daichi Nuclear Power Plant disaster. A group of technologists, scientists, and local communities used "rapid, integrated, open development, simultaneously addressing requirements in several disparate fields, including hardware

**Table 8.1. Projects**

| Project | What is it about? | Images |
|---|---|---|
| Arduino micro-controllers https://www.arduino.cc/ | a family of low-cost circuit boards<br>each board has a core processor, memory, and analog and digital input/output peripherals through which they can sense and affect their immediate surroundings<br>relatively easy to operate and used in many research and education settings, including student lab kits and basic equipment like photogates | 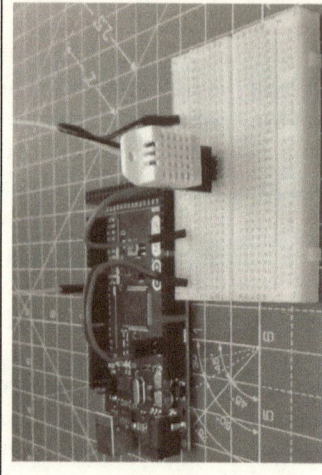<br>**Figure 8.3. A Micro Weather Station: Temperature and Humidity Based on Arduino**<br>*Source:* https://metastudio.org/t/iot-micro-weather-station-temperature-and-humidity/379. |
| Raspberry Pi http://www.raspberrypi.org/ | Raspberry Pi, developed in the United Kingdom by the RASPBERRY PI foundation, started producing minicomputer boards in 2012. Raspberry Pi products include motherboards, personal computers, and peripherals that are inexpensive. | <br>**Figure 8.4. A Raspberry Pi Personal Computer**<br>*Source:* Image credits Nagarjuna G. |

ExpEYES
https://expeyes.in

ExpEYES is an indigenously developed board that allows computer interface for several experiments in physics, electronics, and engineering.

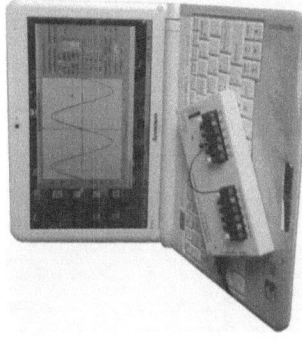

**Figure 8.5. ExpEYES Device with a Laptop**

BeagleBone
http://beagleboard.org/

BeagleBone® AI-64 brings a complete system for developing artificial intelligence (AI) and machine learning solutions. Industry-leading expansion possibilities are enabled through familiar BeagleBone® cape headers, with hundreds of open-source hardware examples.

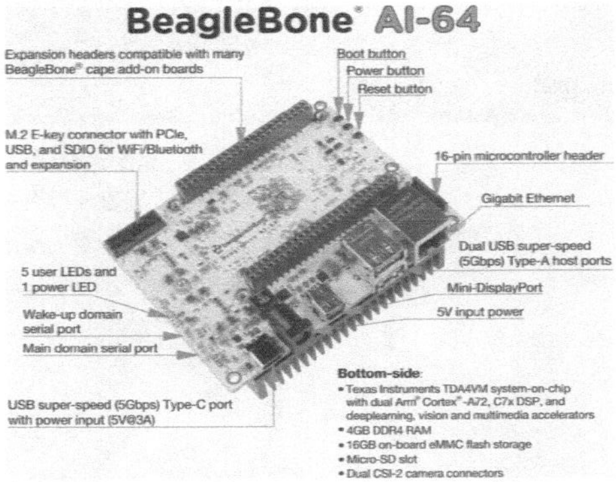

**Figure 8.6. BeagleBone**

*(continued)*

**Table 8.1.** *(Continued)*

| Project | What is it about? | Images |
|---|---|---|
| RepRap 3-dimensional printer<br>https://reprap.org/wiki/RepRap | RepRap takes the form of a free desktop 3-D printer capable of printing plastic objects. Because many parts of RepRap are made from plastic and RepRap prints those parts, RepRap self-replicates by making a kit of itself—a kit that anyone can assemble given time and materials. | 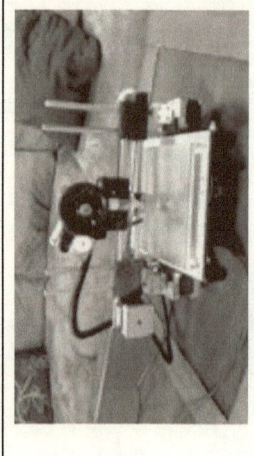<br>**Figure 8.7. Printrbot**<br>License: CC-BY-SA |
| Public Labs<br>https://publiclab.org/ | A project initiated to develop various low-cost sensors and measuring instruments for citizen science with focus on environmental issues. | 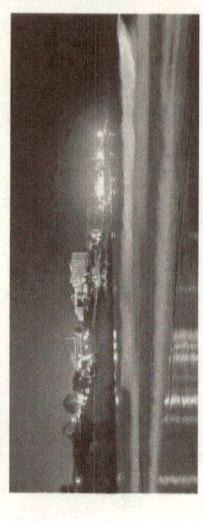<br>**Figure 8.8. Example of Community Science Project Using Public Labs**<br>*Source:* https://publiclab.org/wiki/wateristic-and-underwater-bioluminescence-detector |
| OpenBCI<br>https://openbci.com/ | OpenBCI creates open-source tools for biosensing and neuroscience to lower the barrier to entry for brain-computer interfacing. OpenBCI's latest project is called Galea, a hardware and software platform that merges biometrics with mixed reality in a single headset. | |
| OpenTrons liquid handling robots<br>https://opentrons.com/ | For example, the Opentrons OT-2 robot is an open-source liquid handler designed so that scientists can use it easily. This robot and its accompanying flexible and high-precision automation platform have the ability to automate protocols and workflows in different scientific fields, medicine included. | |

design, software design, engineering, radiation science, visual design and communication, and social design factors." This now means that, if a similar catastrophe should occur again, "more than 1000 of these radiation detectors are in use around the world and the design and documentation is easily accessible for rapid scaling and deployment elsewhere by people with no prior experience building or using radiation monitoring devices" (Parker et al., 2021, p. 11).

The Global South seems to be a fertile ground for open-hardware initiatives and projects. Looking at Fab Labs in Brazil and the Amazon, we note examples such as the first phase of the Amazon Fab Lab project implementation, which focuses on the Peruvian Amazon region of Iquitos.

This first phase included the design of the boat and the fabrication facilities, community research to better understand the existing systems and built environment of Iquitos, and exploring new technologies that can be applied in the community (Velis et al., 2016). For additional examples, consult Sperling et al.'s 2015 "Migratory Movements of Homo Faber: Mapping Fab Labs in Latin America."

Many of the open hardware projects discussed above have been reported in educational research in various contexts. Some of them use these or other open hardware projects to make laboratory equipment or sensors and robots. In education, Raspberry Pi (Yamanoor & Yamanoor, 2017; Balon & Simić, 2019; Soboto et al., 2013; Brock et al., 2013), Ardiuno (Hurtuk et al., 2017; Jamieson & Herdtner, 2015; Kubínová & Šlégr, 2015; Kinchin, 2018; Huang, 2015; Petry et al., 2016), and ExpEYES (Dhakulkar & Nagarjuna, 2015) have been used. Interestingly, some of the providers of open hardware go beyond the hardware to assist with teaching and learning. For example, Raspberry Pi has a web page specifically for teachers (https://www.raspberrypi.org/teach/). It hosts webinars and actively encourages communities to do research in a collaborative way.

Researchers such as Choi and Kim (2022) and Mahmood et al. (2019) confirm what Xiaoyang and Yao (2016) had observed; namely, open hardware in the form of a Raspberry Pi development board or single board computer is useful when it comes to teaching and implementing the Internet of Things (IoT) technologies and environments. According to Flanagan (2020), both the Arduino board and Raspberry Pi are successful open hardware tools to help students acquire certain programming concepts.

Apart from these, robotics has proven to be a fertile entry point for young learners. The fascination of being able to create and control a "robot" seems to be universal. As discussed by Mondada et al. (2017), mobile robots are valuable tools for education because robotics technology is multidisciplinary

**Figure 8.9.** Using ExpEYES Device to Capture Voltage Generated from a DIY Wind Generator. For details of construction, see https://arvindguptatoys.com. (a) The complete generator made from a used plastic bottle and a CD. (b) The placement of coils. (c) ExpEYES device connected to coils. The overlay is the graph from the readings of the device when the generator is set in motion due to wind.
*Source:* Photo by Amit Dhakulkar.

**Figure 8.10.** A Robot Design from metastudio.org. Robotics can be a very fertile entry point for young learners.
*Source:* https://metastudio.org/t/designing-and-building-chotu-bot/3390.

in nature and can be used in a wide range of fields (e.g., complex mechanics, sensors, wireless transmission, mathematics, and computer science). Due to lack of diversity, high cost, noninclusive design, lack of educational material, and lack of stability over time (Mondada et al., 2017), they are not always appreciated in schools and universities.

The Thymio project, described by Mondada et al. (2017), includes "a mature mass-produced open-hardware robot, at a low price, with a multi-age and gender-neutral feature set, and with a design promoting creativity, facilitating learning, and providing a wide range of interaction possibilities from built-in behaviors to text programming, passing through different visual programming environments" and is thus a good example of effective and efficient use of open hardware. Similar examples of open hardware robots conceived, designed, and implemented by a community of users, developers, and manufacturers can be found in the literature (Bertelli et al., 2007; Kochlán & Hodon, 2014; Betancur-Vásquez et al., 2021).

## Discussion

In discussing open hardware for teaching and learning, one of the first things that comes to mind is affordability. In a cost comparison, open hardware will be several times less expensive than its commercial counterparts. But as is the case with OERs and FOSS, having a low cost is just one benefit of open hardware. The main benefit, particularly in the educational context, stems from the idea that designs can be shared freely. As Maia Chagas (2018) correctly observes,

> we don't necessarily need more money but rather need to reassess our relationship to knowledge and technology, how it determines our role in society, and how we want to spend grant money entrusted to us by the people. By making our tools and knowledge truly free, "haves and have nots" will not only erase the divide but will actually move together to a better way.

It is, rather, the way technology (in terms of hardware) is currently employed that is detrimental to several aspects of teaching and learning, and it is felt most acutely by those on the lower end of the economic stratification.

The range of open hardware and open technological devices is impressive, from amateur radio (Homebrew D-STAR Radio), to robots, cameras, gaming consoles (Uzebox), cell phones (ARA Project), and audio equipment (Aurora 224) to desktop and portable computers. For scientific research, both for educational institutions (universities and schools) and industry, there are optical devices, pH meters, spectrometers, centrifuges

(Gibb, 2014; Pearce, 2014), infusion pumps (Wijnen et al., 2014), miniature fluorescence microscopes (Ghosh et al., 2011), and biopotential systems (Open Ephys) (Siegle et al., 2017).

Pearce (2014) systemized the benefits of the OSH paradigm as follows: massive peer-review in the development of material and projects, which leads to improvement of the experimental protocol and hardware project (often with costs radically reduced), which provides equipment with better performance. In addition, OSH leads to increased visibility and therefore citations, which in turn brings about increased funding opportunity and improved (student) recruitment, plus improved student training and education in the field of science.

Ratikin and Markova (2022) and Hannig and Teich (2021) discuss three distinct advantages of open hardware/FOSH over proprietary hardware:

1. *Innovation*: Due to the collaborative nature of development of FOSH and reuse of different works, the overhead can be reduced and better-quality innovations can be actualized.
2. *Sharing of Knowledge*: The knowledge and competence can become available to anyone, without licensing cost or long and costly training.
3. *Confidence and Transparency*: Due to the black box nature of proprietary hardware, there is an uncertainty regarding potential backdoors in the software or firmware and how data (personal and other) is collected. In contrast, FOSH gives transparency, traceability, and security as the source code is available for anyone to examine.

In addition, Kera (2017) emphasizes the democratic and decentralized nature of open hardware and further adds, "While professional scientists use OSH to customize and optimise their instruments, citizen scientists, artists, and various enthusiasts extend the role of these instruments from research to political activism, open exploration, art, and other creative (mis)uses" (p. 97). For this author still, the open movement includes the democratic features of OSH: increased participation, cocreation and collaboration, decentralization of research infrastructure and empowerment in terms of assessing risks, making decisions, and formulating new context-relevant research questions.

Maia Chagas (2018) described the democratic nature of open hardware as allowing "more people to participate in the scientific endeavour, in turn enabling research to be done outside academia, enabling people to exercise their curiosity and better understand the world around them." He also noted that a better understanding of equipment is possible because blueprints can be analyzed and reproduced. Adding the perspective of sustainability, he went on to highlight a clear reduction in vulnerability because there are fewer issues with supply (even if a company stops producing certain devices, research can continue working as they are able to repair or replace those devices).

Finally, Maia Chagas (2018) also links the democratic nature of open hardware to the ease of gathering information about, for example, material costs. This puts researchers, students, and teachers at an advantage when they have to decide on the reasonableness of the price of a certain piece of equipment (perhaps it is a better value to build, calibrate, and repair their own equipment).

When students and teachers build their own equipment, they learn about other scientific areas (e.g., electronics or physics). These interdisciplinary, hands-on "moments" offer additional teaching possibilities for schools and universities, linked to essential twenty-first-century skills such as creativity, innovation, and problem solving.

The Global Open Science Hardware Roadmap (https://openhardware.science/global-open-science-hardware-roadmap/) indicates the following actions for open hardware to become ubiquitous:

- Creating institutional and funding support structures
- Preparing guidelines for hardware designers, funders, users, and newcomers on key aspects of OSH development, such as quality control and standards compliance, licensing, documentation standards, and social and ethical aspects of scientific work
- Involving the members of the OSH community in the task of elaborating an assessment framework for OSH projects
- Using the results of collaborative research to build a common pool of open educational resources
- Creating mentorship programs and support networks to increase diversity in the OSH community

Our task to aid teachers will be to create supporting environments and policies to realize these at the grassroots level for the above-mentioned objectives. As we have proposed in our model earlier (Ferreira-Meyers & Dhakulkar, 2021), it encompasses several facets of the open movement. We propose to use open science principles as a framework to guide teacher professional development. Some components of the proposed model are shown in figure 8.11.

Thus, we are proposing to embed activities for teaching and learning, supported by FOSH and taking place in a maker space environment. The implementation of CoP via maker spaces will create a potentially rich teaching-learning environment with several avenues for teachers to get experience

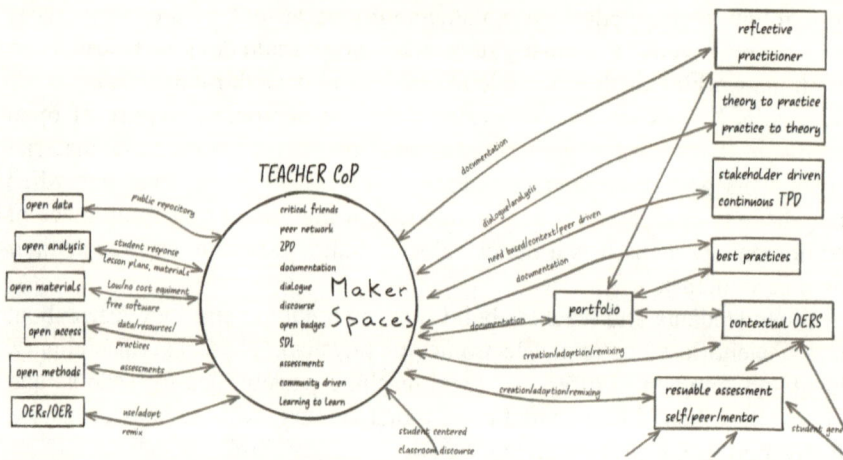

**Figure 8.11. Focus on Teacher CoP**
*Source:* Adapted from Ferreira-Meyers & Dhakulkar (2021).

enacting theories of learning into practice. This hands-on experience, aided by the open science framework, will help spread innovations and create best teaching-learning practices.

Oskay & Barrett (2015) in their amazing work give us a sense of what is possible with such an approach. In our model, everyone has a role to play, as different people will come with different and sometimes complementary skills and knowledge. For example, some teachers may be more knowledgeable in electronics, while others can have subject knowledge or be software experts.

The CoP in the form of a maker space will allow these different skill sets to come together, and participants will have great opportunities to learn from each other. This is a *flexible model* of Vygotsky's zone of proximal development (Dhakulkar et al., 2018) in which the roles of the learner and the mentor are not fixed but change depending on the context of learning. For example, an electronics expert can learn a lot about software from the software expert and vice versa. Thus, the maker space can be a space for a participatory community of practice, where ownership is vested in the members and their shared interests.

## Recommendations

Based on the discussions earlier, we provide recommendations for promoting use of open hardware in teacher education:

- Raise awareness about the benefits of open hardware via hands-on workshops, seminars, and other materials.
- Develop policies that support open hardware CoPs by teachers.
- Both in-service and pre-service teachers should have good exposure and hands-on "tinkering" experience with open hardware.
- Establish best practices for documentation in the context of science hardware with exemplars of use incorporating open educational practices.
- Increase the awareness of CAD editors to open-source hardware and software.
- Provide a two-layer development model for hardware: one for design and one for implementation.
- Research institutions such as universities should recognize, prioritize, and actively support open hardware in the long term.
- Establish maker spaces with community involvement as entry points for open hardware for teachers and students.
- Integrate curricular topics with maker spaces and vice versa.

## CONCLUSION

One of the major challenges to teacher education has to do with lack of financing and other resources for infrastructure and technological innovations. The legal mechanisms (patents and copyrights) to ensure that innovations have the potential to be commercially viable have negative side effects, too: according to Maia Chagas (2018), they increase product development costs (lots of costs are incurred when people try to obtain a patent for their invention/innovation), slow down innovation cycles, create "black box" technologies or innovations (users cannot open them to repair or maintain them or, simply, to understand how they work), and equipment is thrown away instead of being repaired.

The emergence of open and low-cost technologies (e.g., micro-controllers, 3D-printers, sensors, and actuators that enable customized equipment in university and industry laboratories) has made open hardware increasingly popular. As noted by Smith et al. (2017), multiple global movements exist related to open hardware (Fablabs, Hackerspaces, Makerspaces).

Seen as a "modern version of the do-it-yourself (DIY) tradition" (Maia Chagas, 2018), open hardware is useful in the education sector for a variety of reasons, among which we can cite that it assists both teachers and students to become more fluent and expressive with new technologies and to explore concepts in science, mathematics, computer science, and engineering by providing these stakeholders with improved, engaging learning experiences that allow them to design and create objects.

We agree well with the Africa OSH initiative "aims to promote science and innovation in Africa, so as to create innovative solutions that are locally adaptable, culturally relevant, technologically feasible, economically viable, and environmentally sustainable" (http://africaosh.com/). We need more grassroot level initiatives to spread the ideas further and form participatory CoPs especially for people who are traditionally underserved.

Although there are definitely challenges to the use of open hardware—be it for educational purposes or otherwise—for example, legal uncertainty of designing open hardware using professional computer-aided design (CAD) tools and the difficulty to distribute the development (Mondada et al., 2017)—the advantages outweigh the challenges.

## REFERENCES

Balon, B., & Simić, M. (2019). Using Raspberry Pi computers in education. In *2019 42nd International Convention on Information and Communication Technology, Electronics and Microelectronics (MIPRO)* (pp. 671–676). Institute of Electrical and Electronics Engineers (IEEE).

Bertelli, L., Bovo, F., Grespan, L., Galvan, S., & Fiorini, P. (2007). Eddy: An open hardware robot for education. In *4th International Symposium on Autonomous Minirobots for Research and Edutainment (AMIRE)*, Buenos Aires, Argentina.

Betancur-Vásquez, D., Mejia-Herrera, M., & Botero-Valencia, J. S. (2021). Open source and open hardware mobile robot for developing applications in education and research. *HardwareX, 10*, e00217.

Brock, J. D., Bruce, R. F., & Cameron, M. E. (2013). Changing the world with a Raspberry Pi. *Journal of Computing Sciences in Colleges, 29*(2), 151–153.

Choi, S. O., & Kim, J. (2022). Design and implementation of IoT platform education system based on open-source hardware. *International Journal of Software Innovation (IJSI), 10*(1), 1–10.

De Beer, J. (2016). Re-imagining science education in South Africa: The affordances of indigenous knowledge for self-directed learning in the school curriculum. *Journal for New Generation Sciences, 14*(3), 34–53.

De Beer, J. (2019a). Glocalisation: The role of indigenous knowledge in the global village. In J. De Beer (Ed.), *The decolonisation of the curriculum project: The affordances of indigenous knowledge for self-directed learning* (NWU Self-directed Learning Series Volume 2) (pp. 1–23). AOSIS.

De Beer, J. (Ed.). (2019b). *The decolonisation of the curriculum project: The affordances of indigenous knowledge for self-directed learning* (NWU Self-directed Learning Series Volume 2). AOSIS.

Dhakulkar, A., & Nagarjuna, G. (2015). Exploring the transient phenomena of electromagnetic induction. In Sanjay Chandrasekharan et al. (Eds.), *Proceedings of epiSTEME 6: International Conference to Review Research on Science, Technology and Mathematics Education* (pp. 276–284). CinnamonTeal Publishing.

Dhakulkar, A., Shaikh, R., & Nagarjuna, G. (2018). Zone of proximal development in the era of connected computers. In S. Ladage & S. Narvekar (Eds.), *Proceedings of epiSTEME 7: International Conference to Review Research on Science, Technology and Mathematics Education* (pp. 214–221). CinnamonTeal Publishing.

Eriksson, E., Heath, C., Ljungstrand, P., & Parnes, P. (2018). Makerspace in school—Considerations from a large-scale national testbed. *International Journal of Child-Computer Interaction, 16*, 9–15.

Ferreira-Meyers, K., & Dhakulkar, A. (2021). Can open science offer solutions to science education in Africa? In D. Burgos & J. Olivier (Eds.), *Radical solutions for education in Africa* (pp. 149–157). Springer.

Flanagan, M. D. (2020). *Programming education: Using the Raspberry Pi and games to teach programming* (Honors paper). University of Cape Town. https://projects.cs.uct.ac.za/honsproj/cgi-bin/view/2020/flanagan.zip/docs/FLNMAR011_PyPi Game_FP.pdf

Ghosh, K. K., Burns, L. D., Cocker, E. D., Nimmerjahn, A., Ziv, Y., Gamal, A. E., & Schnitzer, M. J. (2011). Miniaturized integration of a fluorescence microscope. *Nature Methods, 8*, 871–878. doi:10.1038/nmeth.1694

Gibb, A. (2014). *Building open-source hardware: DIY manufacturing for hackers and makers.* Addison-Wesley Professional.

Hall, B. L., & Tandon, R. (2017). Decolonization of knowledge, epistemicide, participatory research and higher education. *Research for All, 1*(1), 6–19.

Hannig, F., & Teich, J. (2021). Open-source hardware. *Computer, 54*(10), 111–115.

Heradio, R., Chacon, J., Vargas, H., Galan, D., Saenz, J., De La Torre, L., & Dormido, S. (2018). Open-source hardware in education: A systematic mapping study. *IEEE Access, 6*, 72094–72103.

Huang, B. (2015). Open-source hardware—microcontrollers and physics education—integrating DIY sensors and data acquisition with Arduino. In *2015 ASEE Annual Conference & Exposition* (pp. 26.1205.1–26.1205.13). https://peer.asee.org/open-source-hardware-microcontrollers-and-physics-education-integrating-diy-sensors-and-data-acquisition-with-arduino.pdf

Hurtuk, J., Chovanec, M., & Ádam, N. (2017). The Arduino platform connected to education process. In *2017 IEEE 21st International Conference on Intelligent Engineering Systems (INES)* (pp. 71–76). IEEE.

Jamieson, P., & Herdtner, J. (2015). More missing the boat—Arduino, Raspberry Pi, and small prototyping boards and engineering education needs them. In *2015 IEEE Frontiers in Education Conference (FIE)* (pp. 1–6). IEEE.

Kera, D. (2017). Science artisans and open science hardware. *Bulletin of Science, Technology & Society, 37*(2), 97–111.

Keune, A., & Peppler, K. (2019). Materials-to-develop-with: The making of a makerspace. *British Journal of Educational Technology, 50*(1), 280–293.

Kinchin, J. (2018). Using an Arduino in physics teaching for beginners. *Physics Education, 53*(6), 063007.

Kochlán, M., & Hodon, M. (2014). Open hardware modular educational robotic platform—Yrobot. In *2014 23rd International Conference on Robotics in Alpe-Adria-Danube Region (RAAD)* (pp. 1–6). IEEE.

Kubínová, Š., & Šlégr, J. (2015). Physics demonstrations with the Arduino board. *Physics Education, 50*(4), 472.

Le Grange, L. (2007). Integrating western and indigenous knowledge systems: The basis for effective science education in South Africa? *International Review of Education, 53*(5–6), 577–591.

Le Grange, L. (2016). Decolonising the university curriculum: Leading article. *South African Journal of Higher Education, 30*(2), 1–12.

Mahmood, S., Palaniappan, S., Hasan, R., Sarker, K. U., Abass, A., & Rajegowda, P. M. (2019). Raspberry PI and role of IoT in education. In *2019 4th MEC International Conference on Big Data and Smart City (ICBDSC)* (pp. 1–6). IEEE.

Maia Chagas, A. (2018). Haves and have nots must find a better way: The case for open scientific hardware. *PLoS Biology, 16*(9), e3000014.

Martinez, S. L., & Stager, G. (2019). *Invent to learn: Making, tinkering, and engineering in the classroom* (2nd ed.). Constructing Modern Knowledge Press.

Mersand, S. (2021). The state of makerspace research: A review of the literature. *TechTrends, 65*, 174–186. https://doi.org/10.1007/s11528-020-00566-5

Mersand, S., Gascó-Hernández, M., Gil-Garcia, J. R., Burke, G. B., Figueroa, M., & Sutherland, M. (2018, May). The role of public libraries in smart, inclusive, and connected communities: current and best practices. In *Proceedings of the 19th Annual International Conference on Digital Government Research: Governance in the Data Age* (pp. 1–2).

Mondada, F., Bonani, M., Riedo, F., Briod, M., Pereyre, L., Rétornaz, P., & Magnenat, S. (2017). Bringing robotics to formal education: The thymio open-source hardware robot. *IEEE Robotics & Automation Magazine, 24*(1), 77–85.

Oskay, W., & Barrett, R. (2015). *The annotated build-it-yourself science laboratory: Build over 200 pieces of science equipment!* Maker Media.

Paganelli, A., Cribbs, J. D., "Silvie" Huang, X., Pereira, N., Huss, J., Chandler, W., & Paganelli, A. (2017). The makerspace experience and teacher professional development. *Professional Development in Education, 43*(2), 232–235.

Parker, A., Dosemagen, S., Molloy, J., Bowser, A., & Novak, A. (2021). *Open hardware: An opportunity to build better science.* https://diplomacy21-adelphi.wilsoncenter.org/sites/default/files/media/uploads/documents/STIP%20Open%20Hardware%20An%20Opportunity%20to%20Build%20Better%20Science_0.pdf

Pearce, J. M. (2014). *Open-source lab: How to build your own hardware and reduce research costs.* Elsevier.

Petry, C. A., Pacheco, F. S., Lohmann, D., Correa, G. A., & Moura, P. (2016). Project teaching beyond physics: Integrating Arduino to the laboratory. In *2016 Technologies Applied to Electronics Teaching (TAEE)* (pp. 1–6). IEEE.

Rakitin, I., & Markova, V. I. (2022). Open-source hardware—advantages and applications. In *2021 International Conference on Biomedical Innovations and Applications (BIA)* (Vol. 1, pp. 21–24). IEEE.

Resnick, M., & Rosenbaum, E. (2013). Designing for tinkerability. In *Design, make, play* (pp. 163–181). Routledge.

Santos, B. S. (2015). *Epistemologies of the South: Justice against epistemicide*. Routledge.

Siegle, J. H., López, A. C., Patel, Y. A., Abramov, K., Ohayon, S., & Voigts, J. (2017). Open Ephys: An open-source, plugin-based platform for multichannel electrophysiology. *Journal of Neural Engineering, 14*(4), 045003.

Smith, A., Fressoli, M., Abrol, D., Arond, E., & Ely, A. (2017). *Grassroots innovation movements*. Taylor & Francis.

Sobota, J., PiŜl, R., Balda, P., & Schlegel, M. (2013). Raspberry Pi and Arduino boards in control education. *IFAC Proceedings Volumes, 46*(17), 7–12.

Sperling, D. M., Herrera, P. C., & Scheeren, R. (2015). Migratory movements of homo faber: Mapping fab labs in Latin America. In *International Conference on computer-aided architectural design futures* (pp. 405–421). Springer.

Velis, E., Baptista, P., Brazil, J., Machado, R., Valladares, C., & Waissbluth, N. (2016). Peer-based design, prototyping and construction of a floating fab lab in the Amazon. Paper presented at Fab12, 1.

Wenger, E. (2011). *Communities of practice: A brief introduction*. Retrieved August 12, 2022, https://scholarsbank.uoregon.edu/xmlui/handle/1794/11736

Wijnen, B., Hunt, E., Anzalone, G., & Pearce, J. (2014). Open-source syringe pump library. *PLoS One, 9*, 1–8. doi:10.1371/journal.pone.0107216

Xiaoyang, Z., & Yao, L. (2016). Raspberry Pi: An effective vehicle in teaching the internet of things in computer science and engineering. *Electronics, 5*(3), 56. https://doi.org/10.3390/electronics5030056

Yamanoor, N. S., & Yamanoor, S. (2017). High-quality, low-cost education with the Raspberry Pi. In *2017 IEEE Global Humanitarian Technology Conference (GHTC)* (pp. 1–5). IEEE.

## Chapter Nine

# A Boat on the River

## *The Case of Teacher Autonomy, Professional Development, and Online Communities*

Mandana Arfa-Kaboodvand
and Karen Ferreira-Meyers

The more embedded an intervention is in the organization and culture of a school, the more sustainable an impact it has, moving schools toward a culture of professional learning and collaboration (Admiraal et al., 2021).

Wicked competencies in education are those competencies that are difficult to develop and measure (Knight & Page, 2007); autonomy in education is considered one of these wicked competencies (Holmes, 2018). Despite this challenge, it seems that the general concept of autonomy is favored more than ever in modern education and, therefore, might be here to stay.

Even though different interpretations of autonomy in education have existed throughout time, the emergence and popularity of learner-centeredness in education and language teaching, mainly in the second half of the 20th century, have brought the idea to the forefront; thus, the main goal of modern education is to help learners reach autonomy. In addition, and keeping pace with learner autonomy, the concept of teacher autonomy has attracted considerable attention since the final years of the 20th century. Teacher self-development, self-evaluation, and reflection (Little, 1995; Nunan, 1988) and teachers as "self-directed learner[s] and practitioner[s]" (Benson, 2011, p. 187) are among the concepts in line with their autonomy in education or are believed to make autonomy happen.

Kumaravadivelu's proposed operating principles of "practicality, particularity and possibility" (2012, p. 12) for language teacher education in the global society is a clear example of how teacher education is evolving and encouraging teachers to reflect and decide on their professional development based on the circumstances and contexts in which they live and work. The popularity of reflective and self-development portfolios (Smith & Tillema, 2003) can be seen as another piece of evidence of the importance given to voluntary reflection. Currently, the internet seems to have opened more doors; therefore, endless opportunities are available for teachers autonomously to find the paths that they like or need to pursue.

In this chapter, after briefly reviewing the concept of autonomy in education, we focus on teacher autonomy, paying particular attention to the relationship between autonomy and professional development. We also explore some of the reasons why certain teachers cannot or refuse to reach autonomy in their jobs and pursue professional development. We build on the assumption that autonomy in education is needed and, in order to help learners reach it, teachers should also be willing to be—and know how to be—autonomous.

We end the chapter by examining some solutions, including how online platforms and online communities may assist in the process of affording teachers opportunities to become autonomous.

## WHAT IS AUTONOMY IN EDUCATION?

As mentioned briefly earlier, defining autonomy in education is rather complicated, and reaching a consensus about its meaning is debatable (Wermke & Salokangas, 2015). It is a multidimensional term, and, therefore, it can be examined from very different angles. It has political, philosophical, and pedagogical dimensions and implications. Yet, in many of the definitions, concepts and principles emerge that are inspired by the philosophy of postmodern education, which is to have learners reach a stage where they can set their own goals and look for ways to reach them.

What differs in the definition of autonomy, though, is that some see it as the result of postmodern education whereas others view it as a means to reach the goals that it introduces (Mausethagen & Mølstad, 2015). Another aspect of autonomy concerns what leads to autonomy. It is owning your work and being accountable for it. Pedagogically, the consensus is that autonomous learning programs foster autonomy through encouraging learners to control their learning and making informed decisions (Benson, 2011).

As the Norwegian National Common Core Curriculum for primary and secondary schools powerfully, but ambitiously explains:

> Education shall provide learners with the capability to take charge of themselves and their lives, as well as with the vigour and will to stand by others. Education must teach the young to look ahead and train their ability to make sound choices, allow each individual to learn by observing the practical consequences of his or her choices, and foster means and manners, which facilitate the achievement of the results they aim at. The young must gradually shoulder more responsibility for the planning and achievement of their own education, and they must take responsibility for their own conduct and behavior. (Cited in Trebbi, 2011, p. 42)

School education, then, should support "the individual's development towards autonomy" (Uljens & Rajakaltio, 2017, p. 28). The word "individual" is very meaningful here, as autonomy has different stages and manifests itself differently in each person and context (Hickox & Moore, 1995; Lamb & Reinders, 2008). This multilayeredness of autonomy may be among the reasons for the multiplicity of definitions. Liberal humanism may be the philosophical inspiration for autonomy in education; however, reaching it goes beyond that.

## Teacher Autonomy

Struggling to define and reach autonomy in education is not limited to learners. It is believed and supported by research that learner autonomy depends on teacher autonomy (Little, 1995; Ramos, 2006) and the idea that teachers should be autonomous learners themselves to be able to promote and guide learner autonomy (Manzano Vázquez, 2018).

Like learner autonomy, "teacher autonomy is a complex phenomenon that possesses philosophical, psychological, sociological and historical-political aspects" (Haapaniemi et al., 2021, p. 548).

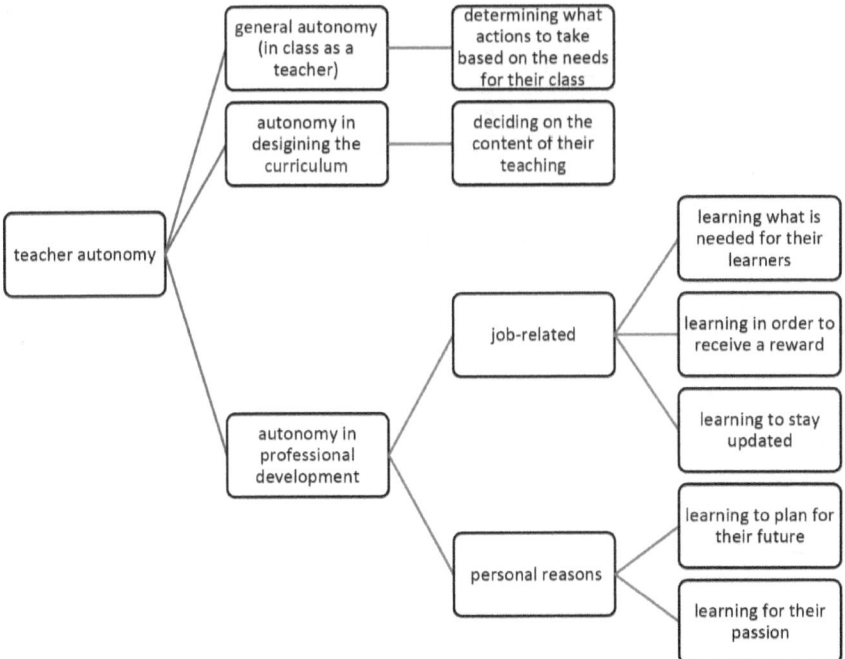

Figure 9.1.  Areas of Teacher Autonomy

Examining the concept of teacher autonomy more closely demonstrates that one dimension that practically all research agrees upon concerns teachers having autonomy within their classes (Wermke et al., 2019). Pearson and Hall (1993, p. 173) call it "general autonomy." It is about the teachers' freedom to select teaching material and teaching methodology. Autonomous teachers are, or are willing, to be responsible for deciding what and how to teach at a given time and place—and act upon that.

The second area demanded for teacher autonomy is curriculum autonomy, which means that teachers would be responsible for, at the very least, participating in designing the curriculum (Pearson & Hall, 1993, p. 173).

The third direction that has more recently engaged the attention of many teachers and researchers (Artman et al., 2020; Canaran & Mirici, 2019; Reeve & Cheon, 2021) and is the focus of this chapter is teachers' autonomy in deciding their professional development path. As Mausethagen and Mølstad (2015, p. 31) clarify, teacher autonomy involves not only freedom of choice, but also "the capacity to grow" and "self-governance."

Autonomy to professionally develop can be based on various factors (figure 9.1) and lead to different outcomes. For instance, sometimes teachers may need to acquire knowledge or learn those skills that they feel are essential for their students' learning or would help them meet their students' demands. At times they may want to acquire new knowledge or skills due to a newfound interest in a topic, possibly based on what they have heard or read. They may also wish to plan their future and seek learning that would help them develop based on how they envisage their future. Some teachers may seek training only to receive some reward, recognition, or promotion.

Others may seek professional development so that they can cope with new circumstances or implement innovations. What happened during the COVID-19 time and how teachers needed to update their knowledge of teaching online is a good example of how need led to professional development in a very limited period of time.

And, finally, a number of teachers may seek professional development out of sheer interest in a topic.

On the whole, autonomy for professional development can be a means of empowering teachers both to function better as educators and to grow and feel in control of their professional lives. And despite their diverse perspectives, different types of autonomy are often closely related, which means that those teachers who professionally develop can perform better in their classes, make informed decisions, have more confidence, and will know how and where to look for answers.

Interestingly, a recent large-scale study conducted by the National Trust Foundation for Educational Research in England suggests that teachers' level of autonomy over their professional development is among the lowest of all the areas of their work. This is despite the fact that self-directed professional development is "the most associated with higher job satisfaction" (Worth & Van den Brande, 2020, p. 3).

Finally, it may seem that general and curriculum autonomy can be the outcome of collective decisions of the teachers alone or of the teachers and the authorities together (Haapaniemi et al., 2021). However, it seems autonomy for professional development stems from the interest or need of each teacher and is more individual than collective in nature (Svendsen, 2020). Later in the chapter, we argue otherwise and suggest that it can still be a collaborative decision.

## Hindrances and Constraints to Teachers' Pursuing Autonomy and Professional Development and Learning

At least on the surface teacher autonomy is very desirable for all stakeholders; teachers will have some independence that they may deem necessary, and institutions will have less responsibility, as some responsibility is delegated to the teachers. The same can apply to teachers setting their own professional development plans as opposed to the organizations deciding what they should learn at a given time; however, in many instances, this is not what happens. Various reasons contribute to this lack of teachers' and authorities' interest in teacher autonomy and teacher professional learning. In this section, we review some of them (figure 9.2, after the discussion of the various aspects).

### Lack of Motivation

To begin with, teachers' lack of motivation can be one of the main reasons for their unwillingness to be autonomous (Zhang et al., 2021).

Lawson (2004) argues that sometimes organizations create the illusion of handing power to the teachers. Teachers' development of certain competencies does not always lead to management support; therefore, the implementation of empowerment strategies may lean toward the latter. This may be one of the reasons why some teachers, consciously or subconsciously, do not have the desire to gain more control over improving their competencies and may wait for the organization to prescribe what to do or even organize the training that they think teachers need to have.

Teachers may just see their autonomy as the illusion of autonomy or the illusion of choice (Federov et al., 2020). Some teachers may go as far as seeing themselves as powerless and may see no hope for the future (Lamb, 2000). At the same time, being autonomous without having the authority to do or change anything can be another major issue. If teachers are held accountable for something over which they have no control, then they may not wish to contribute to improving the existing conditions.

Viewing the issue through the eyes of the authorities can also shed light on the challenges of teacher autonomy. Authorities may not trust teachers' judgment. At the end of the day, management is held responsible for what takes place in the workplace in most contexts. Therefore, both teachers and school heads may prefer to avoid conflict or certain issues even at the cost of not improving the development of their learners.

In line with that trend, we look at how teacher autonomy is interpreted in the context where the teachers work. As far as general professional development is concerned, teachers need to believe that they can use their newly gained skill or knowledge in their classes to facilitate their students' learning; otherwise, they may find it futile to attempt to develop their knowledge and seek fresh ideas. Sometimes the authorities may not encourage the change.

In addition, if teachers are hoping for a promotion or pay rise but realize that it may not happen, then again, they may not be motivated to develop.

Overall, the workplace environment may not be creating the challenge or awareness for the teachers to be autonomous or even seek to improve their performance and thus will not be motivating the teachers to seek professional development (Mattingly, 2018).

*Certain Beliefs*

One major hindrance to teachers' pursuing professional development can be teachers', authorities', or even the society's beliefs. And these beliefs also can be linked to teachers having or lacking motivation to improve their knowledge and skills (Juan & Yajie, 2018; Santos & Miguel, 2019).

Teachers' personal views regarding the role of education in general and their own role in particular can be another reason why some of them lack the desire to be autonomous (Borg, 2003; Hacker & Barkhuizen, 2008). This can sometimes stem from contradictions among several aspects of the environment in which they teach and live. The washback effect of exams is among the most important issues.

In addition, the views of the society in which the teachers work may act as a constraint. If teachers are mainly viewed as child minders more than educators, then they may not be motivated to make changes. This view can particularly be seen in, but not limited to, the classes of younger learners (Harwood & Tukonic, 2016; Moloney, 2010).

All in all, teachers' opinion and perception of their roles as the providers of education, the beliefs of the school authorities, and even the views of society on what is to be taught and how, may contribute to teachers' unwillingness to pursue their professional development or practice what they have learned.

*Lack of Knowledge and/or Confidence*

Even though freedom over deciding how to teach and what to learn at a given time is essential, it is equally important for the teachers to have the ability, confidence, and knowledge to make those decisions. A teacher who is not trained to plan attainable goals may not be able to make wise decisions or take the necessary steps to reach the goals. Then that teacher may prefer not to be autonomous in what to learn.

*Lack of Time*

Lack of time due to having responsibilities in and out of the class, lack of facilities, and issues again in and out of the workplace may also contribute to teachers' not being keen on aiming for professional development or demanding autonomy in and beyond their classes.

*Being Satisfied with the Existing Situation*

Having said all of that, being autonomous is difficult. Being held accountable for actions is challenging, and it can be overwhelming. In a way, it is easier to be given tasks and asked to complete them. Some teachers may simply be satisfied with what they are doing and how they are doing it, and may not necessarily look for change. Self-regulating can even seem unrealistic for some teachers.

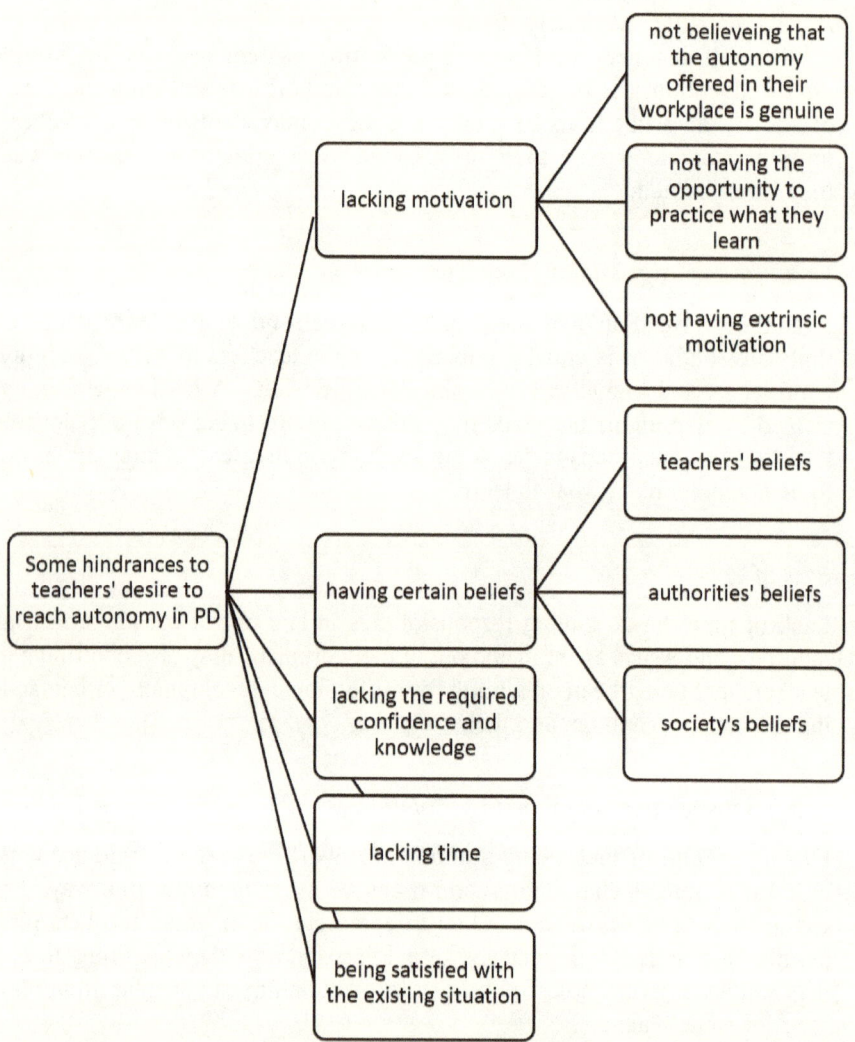

**Figure 9.2.** Hindrances to Teacher Autonomy and Their Desire to Pursue Professional Development

## Discussion and Possible Solutions

Before reviewing possible solutions to these constraints to teacher autonomy, we would like once again to draw on the fact that teacher autonomy is complex and reflects the contexts in which it is applied; therefore, factors outside the classroom and educational institutions play a major role in interpreting and implementing teacher autonomy, if at all.

Autonomy can have different stages. What is considered autonomous teaching in one context may not be seen as autonomous in another. That being said, although all of the hindrances to reaching autonomy are valid, and, in some contexts, due to the prevalent political and social situations, the road to reaching autonomy is more challenging, steps can still be taken to help teachers at least in some aspects of their careers.

For one thing, teacher autonomy does not necessarily contradict control. In Norway for example, the *didaktik* system of curriculum design sets a national curriculum and then gives the teachers and schools the freedom to decide on the process and even outcome of learning. This process can be based on the individual or collective decision of the stakeholders in schools, particularly the teachers (Mausethagen & Mølstad, 2015).

That being said, an educational system that seeks to update its plans and views can better support the teachers and create the environment needed for that. Therefore, a supportive school culture can make a difference in teachers' lives and experiences (Haapaniemi et al., 2021).

The support can range from providing financial reward or recognition, to planning the teachers' time tables in a way that would allow time for professional development and promoting a culture of learning and sharing. The latter stems from, among others, the importance of collaboration in professional development. Rather than being independent, autonomous teachers need interdependence. This comes from dialogue, sharing and interacting with their students, coworkers, and school authorities.

Paulo Freire (1972) went as far as believing that engaging with others makes us human, which constitutes a necessary condition to make choices. This is how professional development leads to professional learning (Freeman, 2002). Interdependence implies "working together with teachers and other learners towards shared goals" (Benson, 2011, p. 15), which means that besides believing in autonomy for themselves, teachers need to cooperate with others when making decisions and solving problems.

Accordingly, learning networks or communities of practice (CoP) as Wenger (2011, p. 1) labels them are "formed by people who engage in a process of collective learning in a shared domain of human endeavor." Teachers can form their own CoPs.

*Online Platforms, Community Building, and Professional Development*

Attending conferences and joining teacher groups and CoPs are very helpful; however, as was discussed earlier, money, time, and other responsibilities can be a major obstacle. And that is how both formal and informal online networking can assist in teachers' professional development (Lantz-Andersson et al., 2018; Oddone et al., 2019; Shelton & Archambault, 2018).

Seeking professional development through online technology is another advantage of having some level of autonomy. It is obviously an alternative to face-to-face learning, and its success, as Wasserman and Migdol (2019, p. 135) put it, depends upon teachers' "acceptance of online learning as an alternative to traditional face-to-face delivery."

The most important advantage of online learning is the level of flexibility and control over learning and learning management, including the time, the amount of time devoted, and the content. Online platforms can cross borders and provide access to resources that might otherwise be unavailable. Teachers can engage in more dialogue with colleagues far and near to widen their horizons and share their experiences.

Online learning can, in many cases, be free of charge and be either formal or informal. It can be synchronous, asynchronous, or hybrid. It can create curiosity and interest and be done individually or in groups. The latter case may lead to recognition by other people in the network. Online learning can even boost the teachers' confidence, particularly when they know the answer to a question or have had an experience like others.

They can be a platform for reflection. They require time management skills, discipline, and high motivation, but autonomous teachers can cope with that. They can also boost autonomy, help teachers improve their time management skills, and create interest in topics they did not know prior to encountering them online.

Internet alone has opened many new doors and opportunities. Massive Online Open Courses (MOOCs) have opened even more doors and access to resources (Koukis & Jimoyiannis, 2019). Using the concept of communities of practice as one potential guiding theme in responding to challenges that science teachers in Africa face led Ferreira-Meyers and Dhakulkar (2021) to seek the value of open science and propose a theoretical model for the African context.

The model also highlights the value of sharing knowledge and adapting the framework to the needs of different teaching and learning communities. Therefore, technology has provided the facilities, and CoPs can help adapt the resources to the contexts. Admiraal et al.'s (2021) study on 14 Dutch secondary school teachers' professional learning communities also supports CoPs' effectiveness. These authors add that "the more embedded an intervention is in the organisation and culture of a school, the more sustainable impact it has, moving schools towards a culture of professional learning and collaboration" (p. 696).

During the COVID-19 pandemic and the restrictions imposed on face-to-face teaching and learning, the necessity to teach and learn online on a day-to-day basis urged many teachers to quest for new ways to approach their students and help them learn and grow. Besides fulfilling their need to teach online, some teachers looked beyond and tried to make sense of the potential of online teaching and assessment.

Everyone recognized the need, and then online platforms and communities assisted in the professional development of the teachers so that they could continue their classes and even sometimes provide higher-quality learning opportunities for their students. Classes during the time of COVID-19 have proven that, in most contexts, some level of teacher autonomy is essential and inevitable.

*Online Communities/Virtual Communities*

CoPs, "virtual communit[ies] of practice" for schoolteachers, as Ghamrawi (2022, p. 5894) puts it, are "often characterized by a population who belong to a bubble of shared interest, and who look forward to learning from one another through social interactions" virtually. Her study with Arab teachers demonstrates that these communities are very helpful for professional development as they encourage collaboration and cooperative problem solving.

Another study conducted by Bett and Makewa (2018) with teachers in Kenya also confirms that, in their teacher-led and informal Facebook groups, teachers learned from each other through answering each other's questions, giving or seeking advice, providing comments, or even sharing a joke. The "sense of togetherness" was what mattered (p. 11).

Another example of an online platform is the Future English Project for language teachers organized by the British Council. According to their website, it "is borderless" and a "digital home for thousands of English language teachers": "They can meet each other, share experience and knowledge, access synchronous and asynchronous learning and document their development in a safe space facilitated by trained facilitators."

Besides the former examples, LinkedIn provides a useful model of an effective online community; it has more than 830 million members, mostly professionals, who mainly network with like-minded professionals and share information, seeking advice and/or commenting on each other's posts.

According to https://www.apollotechnical.com/linkedin-users-by-country/, more than 46 million students and recent graduates are on LinkedIn. LinkedIn has more than 61 million senior-level opinion leaders and 40 million in decision-making positions, making it a top spot for generating leads. And more than one million people publish articles on LinkedIn as influencers creating quality content.

Many teachers across the world are members of WhatsApp and Telegram groups. These groups are sometimes led by teachers and sometimes organized by their institutions. In Turkey, a WhatsApp group created by science teachers "provides field knowledge, shares for pedagogical content knowledge, shares for in-school teaching practices and shares for emotional support" (Cansoy, 2017, p. 285).

All in all, for online communities to be effective platforms for teacher development, teachers should believe in learning online, have some degree of autonomy, have access to the internet, and know how and where to look for information. As Ferreira-Meyers and Dhakulkar (2021, p. 161) emphasize, some mentoring might be needed to "create the use-base for effective participation" among the teachers.

If these needs are met, they will likely take advantage of them. Supportive school environments can be a bonus. Online platforms go beyond borders and provide a ground for sharing and reflecting.

## CONCLUSION AND FINAL THOUGHTS

Teacher autonomy and seeking professional development are closely related. Regardless of the philosophy behind the idea and the varying viewpoints in different contexts, autonomy in education is supposed to accommodate the needs of the individuals and/or the society through helping stakeholders learn to make informed decisions. Teachers can play a major role in assisting learners to reach a certain level of autonomy.

Their perception of autonomy for themselves and the autonomy needed for the students matter and vary from one context to another. Teacher communities can help create and modify their perceptions. And online platforms can be helpful means to assist teachers when they seek information for themselves and for their classes and widen their horizons.

On the one hand, autonomous teachers will be willing to look for help and share information online; and, on the other hand, online platforms and communities can be empowering and help teachers autonomously voice their concerns and grow. Needs, teachers' beliefs, interests, and supportive school environments all contribute to taking advantage of the possibilities that communities and online communities can create.

CoPs can even cross the borders of the teachers' schools and their countries. However, joining the communities needs autonomous teachers and/or a school culture that would promote them.

Creating a teacher community to support teaching and learning can be invaluable even if initiated by the management of an organization; however, maintaining and using it effectively would require passionate teachers who believe in their professionality, their voice, and their interdependence on like-minded people. Then it may be safe to say that a teacher community devoted to continuous professional development can only be sustained if the teachers have some sense of autonomy.

Even if teachers choose to follow the lead of the organization, at least it is the choice that they have made for a reason that they find legitimate. This may suggest that some level of autonomy is better than none, in the sense that the teachers can make better decisions for themselves and their classes, even at micro levels.

Metaphorically, teachers can be compared to sailors. They get on a boat to go from one destination to another. They may just go with the flow of the river; then the water can take them anywhere with a speed that they will have no control over. They may have their oars to help them and give them speed (oars would be their knowledge). The better they know how to use the oars, the easier they can row. If they are with friends who also know how to row, then they may paddle together, and then rowing can be more fun, easier, and faster (friends can be the community).

More important, with friends they can choose which direction to go and not necessarily go with the flow of the river. And if the boat has a sail, then the community has more free time and energy to plan what they want to do when they get to the destination (sails can be the technology). And if they have a navigator or support on land, then they have much more confidence.

If the river branches off, they can make a choice. Wind can sometimes help and sometimes hinder (wind can be the management or the context). But all along the way, it is important for the boaters not to fall out, even if for some reason they do not reach their destination. The boaters should have a plan and be willing to modify it, which suggests that the choices they make and the support they seek matter.

Finally, reaching autonomy is a long path, and the perception of the teachers matters. It is not surprising then that autonomy is a wicked competency. The choices we make and the support we seek matter, too.

## REFERENCES

Admiraal, W., Schenke, W., De Jong, L., Emmelot, Y., & Sligte, H. (2021). Schools as professional learning communities: What can schools do to support professional development of their teachers? *Professional Development in Education, 47*(4), 684–698. https://doi.org/10.1080/19415257.2019.1665573

Artman, B., Danner, N., & Crow, S. R. (2020). Teacher-directed professional development: An alternative to conventional professional development. *International Journal of Self-Directed Learning, 17*(1), 39–50.

Benson, P. (2011). *Teaching and researching autonomy in language learning* (2nd ed.). Pearson Education.

Bett, H., & Makewa, L. (2018). Can Facebook groups enhance continuing professional development of teachers? Lessons from Kenya. *Asia-Pacific Journal of Teacher Education.* doi:10.1080/1359866X.2018.1542662

Borg, S. (2003). Teacher cognition in language teaching: A review of research on what language teachers think, know, believe, and do. *Language Teaching, 36*(2), 81–109. https://doi.org/10.1017/s0261444803001903

Canaran, Ö., & Mirici, İ. H. (2019). An overview of the recent views and practices in teacher professional development. *Eğitimde Kuram ve Uygulama, 15*(4), 350–362.

Cansoy, R. (2017). Teachers' professional development: The case of WhatsApp. *Journal of Education and Learning, 6*(4), 285–293.

Fedorov, A., Ilaltdinova, E., & Frolova, S. (2020). Teachers' professional well-being: State and factors. *Universal Journal of Educational Research, 8*(5), 1698–1710.

Ferreira-Meyers, K., & Dhakulkar, A. (2021). Can open science offer solutions to science education in Africa? In D. Burgos & J. Olivier (Eds.), *Radical solutions for education in Africa* (pp. 149–157). Springer.

Freeman, D. (2002). The hidden side of the work: Teacher knowledge and learning to teach. A perspective from North American educational research on teacher education in English language teaching. *Language Teaching, 35*(1), 1–13.

Freire, P. (1972). *Pedagogy of the Oppressed.* Penguin.

Ghamrawi, N. (2022). Teachers' virtual communities of practice: A strong response in times of crisis or just another fad? *Education and Information Technologies,* 5889–5915. https://doi.org/10.1007/s10639-021-10857-w

Haapaniemi, J., Venäläinen, A., Malin, A., & Palojoki, P. (2021). Teacher autonomy and collaboration as part of integrative teaching—Reflections on the curriculum approach in Finland, *Journal of Curriculum Studies, 53*(4), 546–562. https://doi.org/10.1080/00220272.2020.1759145

Hacker, P., & Barkhuizen, G. (2008). Developing personal theories through reflection in language teacher education. In T. Lamb & H. Reinders (Eds.), *Learner and teacher autonomy: Concepts, realities, and response* (Vol. 1, pp. 161–186). John Benjamins Publishing.

Harwood, D., & Tukonic, S. (2016). Babysitter or professional? Perceptions of professionalism narrated by Ontario early childhood educators. *International Electronic Journal of Elementary Education, 8*(4), 589–600.

Hickox, M., & Moore, R. (1995). Liberal-humanist education: The vocationalist challenge. *Curriculum Studies, 3*(1), 45–59. doi:10.1080/0965975950030103

Holmes, A. G. (2018). Problems with assessing student autonomy in higher education, an alternative perspective and a role for mentoring. *Educational Process: International Journal, 7*(1), 24–38.

Juan, L., & Yajie, C. (2018). EFL teachers' beliefs and practices concerning learner autonomy: A narrative inquiry. *International Journal of Language and Linguistics, 6*(6), 196–201.

Knight, P., & Page, A. (2007). *The assessment of "wicked" competences*. Practice-based Professional Learning Centre, Centre for Excellence in Teaching and Learning, The Open University.

Koukis, N., & Jimoyiannis, A. (2019). MOOCS for teacher professional development: Exploring teachers' perceptions and achievements. *Interactive Technology and Smart Education, 16*, 74.

Kumaravadivelu, B. (2012). *Language teacher education for a global society: A modular model for knowing, analyzing, recognizing, doing, and seeing*. Routledge.

Lamb, T. (2000). Finding a voice: Learner autonomy and teacher education in an urban context. In T. Lamb, I. McGrath, & B. Sinclair, *Learner autonomy, teacher autonomy: Future directions* (pp. 118–127). Longman, Harlow.

Lamb, T., & Reinders, H., Eds. (2008). *Learner and teacher autonomy: Concepts, realities, and response* (Vol. 1). John Benjamins Publishing.

Lantz-Andersson, A., Lundin, M., & Selwyn, N. (2018). Twenty years of online teacher communities: A systematic review of formally-organized and informally-developed professional learning groups. *Teaching and Teacher Education, 75*, 302–315.

Lawson, T. (2004). Teacher autonomy: Power or control? *Education, 32*(3), 3–13. http://dx.doi.org/10.1080/03004270485200261

Little, D. (1995). Learning as dialogue: The dependence of learner autonomy on teacher autonomy. *System, 23*(2), 175–181.

Manzano Vázquez, B. (2018). Teacher development for autonomy: An exploratory review of language teacher education for learner and teacher autonomy. *Innovation in Language Learning and Teaching, 12*(4), 387–398.

Mattingly, P. H. (2018). Workplace autonomy and the reforming of teacher education. In T. S. Popkewitz (Ed.), *Critical studies in teacher education* (pp. 36–56). Routledge.

Mausethagen, S., & Mølstad, C. E. (2015). Shifts in curriculum control: Contesting ideas of teacher autonomy. *Nordic Journal of Studies in Educational Policy, 2015*(2), 28520. https://doi.org/10.3402/nstep.v1.28520

Moloney, M. (2010). Professional identity in early childhood care and education: Perspectives of pre-school and infant teachers. *Irish Educational Studies, 29*(2), 167–187.

Nunan, D. (1988). *The learner-centred curriculum*. Cambridge University Press.

Oddone, K., Hughes, H., & Lupton, M. (2019). Teachers as connected professionals: A model to support professional learning through personal learning networks. *International Review of Research in Open and Distributed Learning, 20*(3), 101–120.

Pearson, L. C., & Hall, B. W. (1993). Initial construct validation of the teaching autonomy scale. *Journal of Educational Research, 86*(3), 172–178.

Ramos, R. C. (2006). Considerations on the role of teacher autonomy. *Colombian Applied Linguistics Journal, 8*, 183–202.

Reeve, J., & Cheon, S. H. (2021). Autonomy-supportive teaching: Its malleability, benefits, and potential to improve educational practice. *Educational Psychologist, 56*(1), 54–77.

Santos, D., & Miguel, L. (2019). The relationship between teachers' beliefs, teachers' behaviors, and teachers' professional development: A literature review. *International Journal of Education and Practice, 7*(1), 10–18.

Shelton, C., & Archambault, L. (2018). Discovering how teachers build virtual relationships and develop as professionals through online teacherpreneurship. *Journal of Interactive Learning Research, 29*(4), 579–602.

Smith, K., & Tillema, H. (2003). Clarifying different types of portfolio use. *Assessment & Evaluation in Higher Education, 28*(6), 625–648, doi:10.1080/0260293032000130252

Svendsen, B. (2020). Inquiries into teacher professional development—What matters? *Education, 140*(3), 111–130.

Trebbi, T. (2011). Language learner autonomy in a Norwegian context. In J. Miliander & T. Trebbi (Eds.), *Educational policies and language learner autonomy in schools: A new direction in language education* (pp. 40–52). Authentik Language Learning Resources.

Uljens, M., & Rajakaltio, H. (2017). National curriculum development as educational leadership: A discursive and non-affirmative approach. In M. Uljens & R. M. Ylimaki (Eds.), *Bridging educational leadership, curriculum theory and didaktik* (pp. 411–437). Springer Open.

Wasserman, E., & Migdal, R. (2019). Professional development: Teachers' attitudes in online and traditional training course. *Online Learning, 23*(1), 132–143. doi:10.24059/olj.v23i1.1299

Wenger, E. (2011). *Communities of practice: A brief introduction.* https://scholarsbank.uoregon.edu/xmlui/bitstream/handle/1794/11736/A%20brief%20introduction%20to%20CoP.pdf

Wermke, W., Olason Rick, S., & Salokangas, M. (2019). Decision-making and control: Perceived autonomy of teachers in Germany and Sweden. *Journal of Curriculum Studies, 51*(3), 306–325.

Wermke, W., & Salokangas, M. (2015). Autonomy in education: Theoretical and empirical approaches to a contested concept. *Nordic Journal of Studies in Educational Policy, 2015*(2), 28841.

Worth, J., & Van den Brande, J. (2020). *Teacher autonomy: How does it relate to job satisfaction and retention?* National Foundation for Educational Research.

Zhang, X., Admiraal, W., & Saab, N. (2021). Teachers' motivation to participate in continuous professional development: Relationship with factors at the personal and school level. *Journal of Education for Teaching, 47*(5), 714–731.

*Chapter Ten*

# Community Facilitation for Social Justice Education

Aspasia Dania*

## INTRODUCTION

Within educational literature, the concept of school reform has received considerable attention in terms of practices that will ensure performance and success in alignment to curriculum and accountability standards (Patterson et al., 2013). However, studies in this field show that it is difficult to put educational policy into school practice.

Embedded cultures within teachers' work, such as school level, parent influences, district or grade level expectations, limit teachers' willingness or ability to enact educational change (Mayer et al., 2015).

As a response to this situation, educational scholars advocate for the establishment of teacher communities as "bottom-up" (Vangrieken et al., 2017) initiatives for empowering teacher professional development. Communities of practice (CoPs), as a specific type of teacher communities, are suggested as relational collectives that can engage teachers effectively in group work with the scope of learning and developing together (Dania & Tannehill, 2022). CoPs position teacher learning as everyday practice and not as top-down skill training (Darling-Hammond & Richardson, 2009).

In this way, they create conditions of democratic, equitable, and sustainable change. CoPs foster trusting exchanges and transfer of tacit knowledge between their members; and they promote learning, mainly through social interactions that are as close as possible to daily work and practice.

For this reason, participation in CoPs is experienced as a process of teacher professional development that is built on a renegotiation of beliefs

---

*School of Physical Education and Sport Science, National and Kapodistrian University of Athens, Greece

and understandings founded on practices of mutual engagement, joint enterprise, and shared repertoires (Lave & Wenger, 1991).

The scope and structure of a community of people sharing a common interest or goal is understood from two perspectives: first, communities as spaces for consolidating individual identity, and second, communities as venues for effective and functional knowledge management. Both perspectives advance the understanding of the importance of collaborative interactions for the achievement of organizational learning and change (Louis & Leithwood, 2021).

What distinguishes CoPs from other types of communities (e.g., learning communities or community networks) is that CoPs are tacitly knit groups of teachers who have developed a coherent and shared identity through their year-long participation in events and activities framed by notions of commitment and belonging to a common mission (Wenger, 1998).

This sense of belonging is based on the assemblages of discourses, people, and regulations within the CoP (Koyama & Varenne, 2012). Thus, when educational discourses call for change, it is easier for teachers to aspire to the need for organizational learning and adapt it to their instructional and pedagogical practices (Wenger, 2010). CoPs function as gatekeepers of shared thinking that eventually validate teachers' efforts and learning toward the assimilation of new policies and practices (Davies, 2005).

By shifting the focus from individual to group learning, CoPs facilitate the coproduction of teacher identity. Within this process, the attainment of teacher change depends more on the outcomes of collaborative interaction, which ultimately validates the importance and impact of shared thinking.

Within CoPs, collaboration may take various forms according to each member's level of participation (Borzillo et al., 2011). Usually, there is a core CoP group whose members are teachers who have worked together for many years and have developed a know-how of things and processes (Dania & Griffin, 2021; Dania & Tannehill, 2022).

The core group members are usually those who share knowledge with novices and can efficiently support the CoP's strategic efforts. Moving outward from the core, active CoP members are regular participants in the CoP events, but they are not as active as the core ones. Active members may be novice or more experienced CoP members who show a presence in all CoP events without wanting or having the time to take leading roles. Finally, peripheral members are those teachers who enter the CoP events only if they are interested, keeping a receiver rather than a producer attitude in terms of socio-material exchange (Dania & Tannehill, 2022).

The coordination of activity events is usually done by CoP facilitators. Facilitators are CoP members or teacher experts (i.e., teacher educators or educational researchers) who commit knowledge, skills, and efforts to the promotion and supervision of the CoP activities and events to ensure that interaction, socialization, and sharing within the CoP remain operative and fruitful for all of its members, despite their position in the CoP circle (Wenger et al., 2002).

In all participation levels, collaborative learning can happen across various domains of interaction, such as the attainment of new positions, the learning of new rituals or routines, or the development of skills in the use of new tools (Cobb & Jackson, 2012). As a result, members usually are given opportunities to move back and forth from the periphery to the CoP core as part of their interaction within face-to-face and virtual discussions, workshops, retreats, and community events. CoPs usually take time to emerge because they must have some form of history to appear.

With the facilitator's guidance, community members share their history and practices and learn to operate with members recognizing one another (Barab & Duffy, 2012; Hoadley, 2012). Those circumstances are necessary for sensitizing teachers to educational policy and change.

The extent to which CoP knowledge and learning will be transformed into improved teacher skills and self-efficacy will depend heavily on the relevance of CoP facilitation initiatives with the scope of teachers' work. Achieving changes in instructional practice requires professional interaction based on content matter and is sustained over time (Poekert, 2011). As such, facilitation to successfully navigate teachers through this process is important. Research has shown that CoP facilitation tasks are central to ensuring CoP performance and success (Hunuk et al., 2019).

Successful facilitation has been described as a process that enables teachers to co-construct new understandings based on their prior skills, experience, and formal knowledge (Parker et al., 2012).

Above all, the facilitator should be knowledgeable and confident enough to use pedagogical strategies for navigating tensions, encouraging interactions, and making space for discussions pertaining to educational policy (Molle, 2013). Strategies of this kind provide structure without dictating, encourage the testing of new ideas, and support teachers in their daily work in practice (Hunuk et al., 2019).

Today's societal challenges (e.g., pandemic outbreaks) and inequalities (e.g., race, class, disability issues) make teachers' work more demanding than previously. The inclusion of pupils who are in danger of being or feeling marginalized remains an issue of concern for many schools that attempt to adopt a social justice agenda for dealing with educational discriminations. The most important aspects of teachers' work on social justice are

- the understanding of curriculum as a living entity,
- appreciation of teaching as a personal and vulnerable process of becoming, and
- empowerment to keep practicing with a social justice orientation (Reyes et al., 2021).

Research has shown that, within CoPs, teachers find it helpful and relevant to engage in participatory action research for gaining understanding of the meaning of social justice and developing the competences needed to teach for social justice (Zollers et al., 2000). Thus, teacher participation in CoPs becomes rather timely.

Based on that, the aim of this chapter is to showcase the importance of the facilitator's role in the development and sustainment of a collaborative CoP climate that focuses on teacher professional development.

By considering social justice as a fundamental concept in educational discourse, an indicative example is given of CoP facilitation strategies that could be used as means of empowering teachers in social justice education. In the following sections, the idea of facilitating a CoP for social justice is presented through several perspectives: (a) the nature of facilitation tasks within a CoP, (b) facilitation along the different phases of CoP members' integration, and (c) CoP facilitation strategies for social justice education.

## The Nature of Facilitation Tasks within a Community of Practice

Social learning theories study learning as a situated and collective enterprise that is mediated by cultural and sociohistorical artifacts and symbols (e.g., language) (Wenger, 2010). Learning within CoPs frames teacher interaction as a social process of developing understandings embedded in collaborative work. CoPs are not sites of narrowly defined activities or practices. Instead, CoP participation means mastery and appropriation of educational policy as a dialectic between the individual and the social (Giddens, 1984).

Traditionally, teachers prefer to work individually and find it difficult to maneuver to social learning practice (Guskey, 2002). The way that CoP learning opportunities are designed will ultimately influence teachers' disposition to collaborative work. Research has shown that even though teachers may influence each other's work within the CoP, this does not always mean that all teachers will seek opportunities to apply things learned outside the CoP (Dania & Tannehill, 2022).

Teachers need to feel empowered—even during minute interactions—to apply CoP knowledge in their practice. It is important, therefore, for teacher interaction within CoPs to be framed on processes of participatory and guided appreciation, as well as apprenticeship training in new instructional models and practices (i.e., as a combination of professional and classroom training) (Dania & Griffin, 2021).

CoP facilitation is instrumental in helping teachers adopt an inquiry stance in teaching (Hadar & Brody, 2021), get access to resources and advice that scaffold learning (Naude & Bezuidenhout, 2015), seek and recognize opportunities for professional development on an ongoing basis, and sustain collegiality as a shared mission for meaningful practice (Assen & Otting, 2022).

Group and/or community facilitation is about "helping groups do better" (Schuman, 2005, p. 3), by focusing on groups and processes, in terms of how things are done, instead of what is done (Brown & Grant, 2010).

The ultimate purpose is to promote values of equality, opportunity, power sharing, and responsibility that are fundamental to the establishment of full cooperation among members. In many circumstances, the facilitator assumes an organizational role and is chosen by CoP members as the person who has the time, energy, and knowledge to keep persevering and/or chasing what CoP members aspire to as a goal (Parker et al., 2012).

In other instances, facilitators may also provide support both in terms of content and process, seeking to create a safe and effective learning and working environment. The facilitator can work as a "CoP designer" who helps the group work and stay focused toward the right direction. However, the role that facilitators will finally adopt depends on the situation (Patton et al., 2012), its contextual boundaries (Huizinga et al., 2015), and the facilitator's preferences (Huizinga et al., 2013).

In the study of Huizinga et al. (2013), teachers' limitations in terms of curriculum design expertise (e.g., especially in connecting assessment with curriculum goals), pedagogical content knowledge (e.g., designing activities based on combinations of skills and knowledge), and curricular consistency expertise (e.g., establishing visions for teamwork) were effectively handled under the facilitator's guidance. Relevant research confirms that the facilitator's role is better enacted when the facilitator is not a natural leader in the team (Truijen et al., 2013).

In such cases, the facilitator can provide both proactive (helping in the design of products or processes) and reactive (following the team's results) support. Ultimately, the alignment of teachers' and facilitators' preferences for support is vital for preventing conflicts and misunderstandings.

To empower teacher learning and change, attention should be paid on facilitation tasks relating to *teacher practice*, *value creation* within the CoP, collaboration as *identity development*, and CoP *organizational issues* (Vrieling et al., 2019). The nature of these tasks is described in the following paragraphs.

*Facilitation and Teacher Practice*

The practical aspect of teacher work is pivotal in the development of strong relationships between individual and shared knowledge. Thus, facilitators should invest in empowering teachers to engage in group work for developing new practices or for creating amendments to existing ones. Teachers' level of participation in the CoP or amount of time invested in CoP activities cannot be determined beforehand. Thus, it is important for facilitators to use available time effectively and help participants learn both formally and opportunistically within group learning situations.

Enhancing individual and group autonomy is important. For example, facilitators could oversee the implementation of blended learning pedagogy workshops, where CoP members may interact face-to-face as well as watch others interacting. In both cases, practice is the overarching theme, while attention is paid to the optimization of appropriate circumstances (e.g., the blended learning workshop format makes participation feasible to all).

Further, facilitators could work with pre- and in-service teachers in school practicums, to help both groups of teachers gain peer-teaching experience within authentic learning circumstances. Giving high challenges and support in practice, observation, and self-assessment activities are issues also important for empowering teachers to adopt a "learning to learn" attitude.

*Facilitation and Value Creation*

Value creation comes from the sharing of ideas and experience among CoP members and the establishment of strong networking bonds. Thus, facilitators should care for the development of an inquiry learning culture, within which objectives and action are negotiated. Dialogue and questioning practices are needed for enabling partnerships and relationships of mutual trust. Within CoP discussions and meetings, facilitators should allow each member to share "ownership" both in problem statement and problem solution.

In every case, it is important that facilitators articulate their own professional knowledge and act as role models in terms of sustaining a practitioner-researcher stance. Participatory action research projects enable facilitators to be perceived as equal CoP members, leading to increased CoP effectiveness and collaborative professional learning (Dania & Griffin, 2021). Research has also shown that when facilitation is enacted with an insider attitude (e.g., CoP members perceive the facilitator as a critical friend and not as an externally imposed leader), critical companionship and scientific knowledge translation are enabled (Dania & Tannehill, 2022; Manley & Titchen, 2017).

## Facilitation and Identity Development

CoP teachers' identity development is pivotal in the establishment of a common mind-set toward achieving rewarding success for all goals. It is important that facilitators care for the sustainment of effective ways of working, along with strengthening teachers' capabilities to match goals, frameworks, and vision concerning their work. Thus, the cultural and belief backgrounds of CoP participants should be considered, and hierarchical structures or critiques of practical and/or theoretical knowledge should be discouraged.

Facilitators should rely on a variety of sources of evidence, experiences, and perspectives to promote spontaneous teacher learning and feelings of belonging (Meirink et al., 2010). For example, group conversations interwoven with individual task assistance and real-time feedback, the use of a wide range of styles for recognizing and praising individual effort, or the employment of various processes (e.g., seminars, workshops, online forums) and skills (e.g., storytelling, writing, demonstrating) for matching participants' level of knowledge and working habits can be helpful for promoting identity development in a deliberate way.

## Facilitation and Organizational Issues

Organizational issues should be taken into consideration as early as the establishment of a CoP. Organization concerns the distribution between directed and self-organized learning activities, local or global initiatives, as well as group and individual priority goals. Facilitators should care for the gradual increase in teachers' self-regulation so that they become able to act locally and disseminate globally (Dania & Griffin, 2021).

The use of a variety of cognitive and creative learning approaches is suggested as a route to integrating CoP knowledge in professional artistry and praxis. This means that facilitators should first understand why teachers participate in the CoP and, based on this understanding, suggest different activities that align with teachers' intentions. For example, networking meetings (face-to-face or virtual) may be relevant for teachers who are interested in interacting with colleagues, whereas learning events (e.g., workshops, discussions, meetings) may be more appropriate to those who seek knowledge expansion. Social events and skill development initiatives (e.g., practical micro-teaching seminars) may align with goals pertaining to the development of social capital, but formal meetings or speeches may be the right events for those seeking to get involved in policy-making initiatives.

## Facilitation along the Different Phases of Community Members' Integration

As already explained, teachers choose to participate in CoPs at different levels according to contextual circumstances or limitations (Wenger et al., 2002). Therefore, facilitation tasks should align with teachers' levels of participation to produce desired outcomes.

Facilitators may act as information experts, inspirators, public managers, guides, or investigators, so that positive attitudes toward the CoP are nurtured. The core group members are usually the people who will mobilize and preserve CoP communication toward strategic objectives while ensuring that the focus remains on a shared repertoire of practices.

Thus, facilitators could help core participants align CoP activities and products to individual and group expectations of mutual benefit. This may mean that facilitators will have to work toward eliminating potential language or cultural barriers, mobilize time and knowledge resources, ensure smooth and relevant discussions and/or contributions among CoP members, or help core members disseminate community events by making the CoP more visible (e.g., online postings, email lists, posters with community events).

For active CoP members, facilitation may focus on the promotion of ownership and the encouragement of responsibility. This may mean that the facilitator is always available to answer members' concerns, respond to requests, and help members initiate contact and share experience, assist in the creation of comfort with the use of CoP resources (e.g., technology, social media), and come up with suggestions for encouraging independent work and rapport.

For active members, facilitation may be experienced more as moderation and supervision to ensure that "burning issues" remain feasible and CoP processes are effectively regulated. Finally, facilitators should care for the development and implementation of CoP initiatives, giving the opportunity for peripheral members to be more active. Peripheral CoP members usually prefer to overhear what is happening within the CoP, and when they become aware of topics of their interest, they decide to participate more actively (Dania & Griffin, 2021).

Thus, facilitators should reassure that access to CoP events or initiatives is provided to all on a regular basis (e.g., through newsletters) and new subtopics or subpractices complement already existing ones. These initiatives could trigger peripheral members to participate or to take the lead in small learning activities, either coming up with their own suggestions or simply gathering information from these sources.

## CoP Facilitation Strategies for Social Justice Education

The facilitator is indeed a central figure regarding CoP communication and interaction. Patterns of interaction within a community play a key role in members' socialization and integration to the common good. Especially when the common good is members' sensitization on social justice education, facilitators should care for those aspects of group dynamics that will keep interaction going. Toseland and Rivas (2005) suggest the term *maypole interaction*, presenting the community leader as a central figure around whom interaction occurs between members in an unhindered way.

Our suggestion is that individual member initiatives should be the maypole of CoP interactions, with the facilitator ensuring that certain aspects of group dynamics are addressed.

In the example of social justice education, the emotional bonds between members are important in sustaining the CoP's cultural and social values toward equity and justice. Rigid norms or hierarchically assigned roles may undermine individual members' skills or dynamics and put control on their autonomy toward reinforcing the CoP's goals.

For teachers aspiring to work with social justice, such an experience may create negative feelings. Thus, facilitation should invest in activities that balance the "control-autonomy paradox" inherent in all collegial relationships. Such activities should give space for negotiation, interpretation, and selective appropriation of decisions, resources, or CoP policy.

CoP participation for social justice should be experienced as a sustained pursuit of learning about teaching that foregrounds ethical concerns, and seeks to adopt an activist orientation toward mechanisms of oppression. Strategies that could enable the attainment of such an experience are presented in the following list:

- *Decentering of privileged communication or interaction practices within the CoP.* Facilitators should provide space for the initiation of affirmative or potentially transformative CoP interaction patterns while directing members' action toward achieving outcomes that are dependent on collective needs.
- *Encouraging active listening and members' openness to uncertainty.* CoPs that invest in social justice education should recognize that most inequalities and injustices in education are perpetuated by the lack of active listening or empathetic thinking. Thus, facilitators should welcome CoP discussions within which members are expected to disclose personal incidents or feelings in a climate of mutual trust. Such discussions offer perspectives of the "other" and establish professional practice as vigilance for shared responsibility.

- *Encouraging humility and intellectual curiosity.* Facilitators should recognize that CoP interaction is to be set up to move teachers toward practice that formulates their limitations and possibilities for change. Thus, one of the challenges that they may experience is the reluctance on the part of some teachers to acknowledge their moral or epistemic responsibility or capacity for change. Many teachers may feel unprivileged or less motivated in their practice in comparison to others and thus adopt a negative stance toward change (Dania & Tannehill, 2022). This stance may be further reinforced when, within CoP meetings, some members dominate in discussions or arguments. The facilitator should take a firm stance against dominating behavior and care for the proceeding of dialogue with the least possible "fanfare" (Zembylas, 2020). Some strategies for achieving this are the initiation of conversations about how people feel in certain circumstances, what needs to be done to feel otherwise (if this is expected), what are the critical conditions for distinguishing responsibility from fault or blame, or what it means to act for reviewing praxis and resisting dichotomized regimes when it comes to educational practice (e.g., white/black, men/women, poor/rich, able/disabled).

## CONCLUDING THOUGHTS

Communities of practice are recognized for their potential to support teachers in terms of their professional growth (Atencio et al., 2012). By intertwining power and knowledge, CoPs nurture relational forms of work and expression to address teachers' professional and personal challenges. Through a sociocritical lens, this approach is beneficial, as it captures aspects of experiencing, sharing, and managing together as fundamental to professional development.

Elements of a CoP's success are dependent on the facilitator's ability to balance knowledge exchange and interaction among CoP members in ways that are conductive to the sustainment of a mobilizing, yet professionally rewarding culture. Different elements of teacher expertise along with the fluidity of relationships and knowledge flows may create barriers to the community's expected outcomes (e.g., production of resources or establishment of mutually supportive interactions).

As such, facilitators should have those skills and knowledge for responding to challenges in respect to the CoP's characteristics (Wenger et al., 2002). Trust among members, as an essential element of CoP belonging, should be facilitated across three basic dimensions: teachers' perceived competence, integrity of interaction, and member benevolence as a priority (Usoro & Majewski, 2011).

Independent of each teacher's decision to affiliate with a CoP, the facilitator should strive for enabling tacit and explicit knowledge to flow in ways that each teacher's habits or (passionate) dispositions are nurtured. As the CoP develops and is recreated, it is expected that some members will leave while others join and regenerate the core or the periphery. Because the prestige of a CoP may depend on the number of people who affiliate with its goals and rationale, the facilitator should work with core CoP members to ensure smooth transitions and relevant contributions, essential knowledge, and skill sharing.

Concerning social justice education, it may be possible that power structures or regional cultures within school communities make teachers' work rather demanding. CoPs can be one of the most appropriate frameworks for supporting teachers in social justice education, provided that all CoP members are encouraged to move back and forth from the peripheries of their shared expertise and individual beliefs. The most important contribution of CoPs toward this objective is the engagement of teachers in critical conversations and praxis for understanding the way(s) that educational discourses/practices produce or sustain inequalities.

Indicative examples are CoP speeches on discrimination in education, workshops on social justice instruction, or the creation of networks for disseminating social justice educational practices. Even though substantial commitment and resources are needed for this purpose, facilitators could support teachers' work/effort using digital resources and blended learning formats of interacting.

Professional learning and freedom for outspokenness are features that take time to develop in teachers' work. However, if the ultimate purpose is the strengthening of professional attributes—such as like-mindedness, cooperation, reciprocity—then the investment in CoP initiatives is a worthwhile endeavor. Especially when teachers' work is directed toward social justice educational goals, attention should be paid to the support of CoP facilitators to create and maintain CoP identity structures of great professional influence.

## REFERENCES

Assen, J. H. E., & Otting, H. (2022). Teachers' collective learning: To what extent do facilitators stimulate the use of social context, theory, and practice as sources for learning? *Teaching and Teacher Education, 114*, 103702.

Atencio, M., Jess, M., & Dewar, K. (2012). "It is a case of changing your thought processes, the way you actually teach": Implementing a complex professional learning agenda in Scottish physical education. *Physical Education & Sport Pedagogy, 17*(2), 127–144.

Barab, S. A., & Duffy, T. M. (2012). From practice fields to communities of practice. In D. H. Jonassen & S. M. Land (Eds.), *Theoretical foundations of learning environments* (2nd ed., pp. 29–65). Routledge.

Borzillo, S., Aznar, S., & Schmitt, A. (2011). A journey through communities of practice: How and why members move from the periphery to the core. *European Management Journal, 29*(1), 25–42.

Brown, S. W., & Grant, A. M. (2010). From GROW to GROUP: Theoretical issues and a practical model for group coaching in organisations. *Coaching: An International Journal of Theory, Research and Practice, 3*(1), 30–45. https://doi.org/10.1080/17521880903559697

Cobb, P., & Jackson, K. (2012). Analyzing educational policies: A learning design perspective. *Journal of the Learning Sciences, 21*(4), 487–521.

Dania, A., & Griffin, L. L. (2021). Using social network theory to explore a participatory action research collaboration through social media. *Qualitative Research in Sport, Exercise and Health, 13*(1), 41–58.

Dania, A., & Tannehill, D. (2022). Moving within learning communities as an act of performing professional wellbeing. *Professional Development in Education*, 1–16.

Darling-Hammond, L., & Richardson, N. (2009). Research review/teacher learning: What matters. *Educational Leadership, 66*(5), 46–53.

Davies, B. (2005). Communities of practice: Legitimacy not choice. *Journal of Sociolinguistics, 9*(4), 557–581.

Giddens, A. (1984). *The constitution of society*. University of California Press.

Guskey, T. R. (2002). Professional development and teacher change. *Teachers and Teaching, 8*(3), 381–391.

Hadar, L. L., & Brody, D. L. (2021). Interrogating the role of facilitators in promoting learning in teacher educators' professional communities. *Professional Development in Education, 47*(4), 599–612.

Hoadley, C. (2012). What is a community of practice and how can we support it? In D. H. Jonassen & S. M. Land (Eds.), *Theoretical foundations of learning environments* (2nd ed., pp. 286–299). Routledge.

Huizinga, T., Handelzalts, A., Nieveen, N., & Voogt, J. (2013). Teacher involvement in curriculum design: Need for support to enhance teachers' design expertise. *Journal of Curriculum Studies, 46*(1), 33–57.

Huizinga, T., Handelzalts, A., Nieveen, N., & Voogt, J. (2015). Fostering teachers' design expertise in teacher design teams: Conducive design and support activities. *Curriculum Journal, 26*(1), 137–163.

Hunuk, D., Tannehill, D., & Levent Ince, M. (2019). Interaction patterns of physical education teachers in a professional learning community. *Physical Education and Sport Pedagogy, 24*(3), 301–317.

Koyama, J. P., & Varenne, H. (2012). Assembling and dissembling: Policy as productive play. *Educational Researcher, 41*(5), 157–162.

Lave, J., & Wenger, E. (1991). *Situated learning: Legitimate peripheral participation*. Cambridge University Press.

Louis, K. S., & Leithwood, K. (2021). From organizational learning to professional learning communities. In K. Leithwood and K. Seashore Louis (Eds.), *Organizational learning in schools* (pp. 275–285). Taylor & Francis.

Manley, K., & Titchen, A. (2017). Facilitation skills: The catalyst for increased effectiveness in consultant practice and clinical systems leadership. *Educational Action Research, 25*(2), 256–279.

Mayer, A., Woulfin, S., & Warhol, L. (2015). Moving the center of expertise: Applying a communities of practice framework to understand coaching in urban school reform. *Journal of Educational Change, 16*(1), 101–123.

Meirink, J., Imants, J., Meijer, P. C., & Verloop, N. (2010). Teacher learning and collaboration in innovative teams. *Cambridge Journal of Education, 40*, 161–181.

Molle, D. (2013). Facilitating professional development for teachers of English language learners. *Teaching and Teacher Education, 29*, 197–207.

Naude, L., & Bezuidenhout, H. (2015). Moving on the continuum between teaching and learning: Communities of practice in a student support programme. *Teaching in Higher Education, 20*(2), 221–230.

Parker, M., Patton, K., & Tannehill, D. (2012). Mapping the landscape of communities of practice as professional development in Irish physical education. *Irish Educational Studies, 31*(3), 311–327.

Patterson, J. A., Campbell, J. K., Johnson, D. M., Marx, G., & Whitener, M. (2013). Using policy attributes theory to examine comprehensive school reform implementation in two Title I middle schools. *Planning and Changing, 44*(1/2), 36.

Patton, K., Parker, M., & Neutzling, M. (2012). Tennis shoes required. *Research Quarterly for Exercise and Sport, 83*(4), 522–553.

Poekert, P. (2011). The pedagogy of facilitation: Teacher inquiry as professional development in a Florida elementary school. *Professional Development in Education, 37*(1), 19–38.

Reyes, G., Aronson, B., Batchelor, K. E., Ross, G., & Radina, R. (2021). Working in solidarity: An intersectional self-study methodology as a means to inform social justice teacher education. *Action in Teacher Education, 43*(3), 353–369.

Schuman, S. (2005). *The IAF handbook of group facilitation: Best practices from the leading organization in facilitation.* Jossey-Bass.

Toseland, R. W., & Rivas, R. F. (2005). *An introduction to group work practice* (5th ed.). Allyn and Bacon.

Truijen, K. J. P., Sleegers, P. J. C., Meelissen, M. R. M., & Nieuwenhuis, A. F. M. (2013). What makes teacher teams in a vocational education context effective? A qualitative study of managers' view on team working. *Journal of Workplace Learning, 25*(1), 58–73.

Usoro, A., & Majewski, G. (2011). Intensive knowledge sharing: Finnish Laurea lab case study. *Vine, 41*(1), 7–25.

Vangrieken, K., Meredith, C., Packer, T., & Kyndt, E. (2017). Teacher communities as a context for professional development: A systematic review. *Teaching and Teacher Education, 61*, 47–59.

Vrieling, E., van den Beemt, A., & de Laat, M. (2019). Facilitating social learning in teacher education: A case study. *Studies in Continuing Education, 41*(1), 76–93.

Wenger, E. (1998). Communities of practice: Learning as a social system. *Systems Thinker, 9*(5), 2–3.

Wenger, E. (2010). Communities of practice and social learning systems: The career of a concept. In *Social learning systems and communities of practice* (pp. 179–198). Springer.

Wenger, E., McDermott, R., & Snyder, W. (2002). *Cultivating communities of practice: A guide to managing knowledge.* Harvard Business School Press.

Zembylas, M. (2020). The biopolitical function of disgust: Ethical and political implications of biopedagogies of disgust in anti-colonial education. *Teaching Education, 33*, 1–16.

Zollers, N. J., Albert, L. R., & Cochran-Smith, M. (2000). In pursuit of social justice: Collaborative research and practice in teacher education. *Action in Teacher Education, 22*(2), 1–14.

# Conclusion

## Passion, Action, Collaboration, and Reflection: Imperative Insights for Teacher Collectives

Sally Wai-Yan Wan

This book offers a very comprehensive and complex framework in searching for and looking into the meanings and functions of "teacher collective" in a multilayered analytic way. Teacher collectives are key drivers to leverage educational change, school improvement, and therefore student learning. Four key underpinning factors affect the growth and development of teacher collectives and determine the extent to which teacher collectives take place: passion, action, collaboration, and reflection.

### PASSION

As stated in chapter 9 of this volume,

> Creating a teacher community to support teaching and learning can be invaluable even if initiated by the management of an organization; however, maintaining and using it effectively would require passionate teachers who believe in their professionality, their voice, and their interdependence on like-minded people. Then it may be safe to say that a teacher community devoted to continuous professional development can only be sustained if the teachers have some sense of autonomy. (p. 147)

The root of teaching is passion, which drives teachers and teacher educators to take challenges and move forward in an uncertain, dynamic, and complex educational landscape (Bernard, 2002; Day, 2004). Unlike cold-blooded machines, teachers are professionals with intrinsic motivation and enthusiasm in teaching and assisting in nurturing and cultivating student potentials and agency in both explicit and implicit learning spaces (Robertson et al., 2020).

This "aesthetic" dimension of looking at teacher identity should not be neglected (Hobbs, 2012).

Apparently, there are mutual impacts between teachers and students in formal and informal interactions (Chang-Tik & Goh, 2020). Cognitive and socioemotional exchanges of experiences lead to personal and professional growth of teachers who are more conscious and aware of variables in the learning environment and adaptive to incorporating a variety of pedagogical strategies to stimulate, strengthen, and support student learning. Teacher commitment and dedication to student learning is to thread the needle to link and connect curriculum, pedagogies, and classrooms intellectually and affectively, where the sociocultural processes of "embodiment" illuminate the ways teachers act, think, and talk (Hayashi & Tobin, 2015).

Passion is certainly vital to the ultimate goal of education—developing students. That said, many past studies (e.g., Tsang, 2019) largely studied teacher demoralization and retention; the sociocultural factors related to policies and workplaces were examined, and these factors would determine or predict teachers' decision to leave (or stay in) the teaching profession due to job dissatisfaction and negative emotions arising from demanding yet unsupportive and paradoxical working environments (Fransson & Grannäs, 2013; Hargreaves, 2005; Ng et al., 2018; Sheridan, 2019; Zhu et al., 2020).

Very limited studies have investigated the ignition, growth, and sustainability of teachers' passion in teaching, where positioning teachers and their identity development can be respectfully and reflexively explored and elicited with acknowledgment of their efforts and relationships with different stakeholders in a broader environment—schools and communities (Hazari et al., 2015; Søreide, 2006; Waitoller & Kozleski, 2013). Grouping passionate teachers—a form of teacher collective—can reinvigorate, reenergize, and reinforce the community's (new) direction and goals, innovative practice, and in-depth exploration of educational meanings through establishing stronger emotional bonds and ties among teachers (Lieberman, 2000; Owen, 2014, 2015, 2016; Sheridan, 2019).

## ACTION

Action is more important than words. With passion, teachers take action and engage in making their dreams come true with a directional compass toward achieving goals. As a key concept of teacher collectives, action research plays a significant role in driving change along the way of expanding learning opportunities and generating knowledge through implementation. Significantly, "action" in action research conducts studies related to learning and teaching for improving the quality of education, where teachers investigate, experiment, and evaluate the effectiveness of curriculum implementation (such as testing new pedagogical ideas). This is the mutual "learning by doing" process, where teachers position themselves as co-learners in action research; it gives "double-loop" feedback to enhance their professional development and create capacity building for school development.

The success of transformative, sustainable change for school improvement and student learning can be guaranteed much more through the simultaneous and collective processes of engaging in participatory research (Souto-Manning, 2012) and taking evidence-based action to promote professional practice and guide curriculum development (Colucci-Gray et al., 2013). During the "learning-by-doing" process, the formation of teacher collectives enables and embraces the development of this learning environment for teachers to construct and build on existing knowledge creatively. Importantly, action research should not be limited to personal classrooms; rather, it can be in the form of cross-classroom of the same grade level, cross-grade levels, cross-subject, cross-school, and even cross-countries. Teacher learning in teacher collectives, therefore, can occur within and/or beyond teachers' schools, regions, and countries (James & McCormick, 2009; Somekh & Zeichner, 2009).

## COLLABORATION

In line with action research, collaboration is another important concept in "teacher collectives." This book has explored the concept of "knobs," where the possibility of "school-university partnership" (Tsui & Law, 2007) can be further discussed in exploring the concept of "teacher collective," where how teachers as practitioners work with university scholars as experts can be investigated accordingly. Past literature illustrated that school-university partnership as a professional learning network is an effective way to facilitate curriculum change and support teacher professional growth. School-university partnership programs have commonly appeared in the form of collaborative action research (Catelli et al., 2000; Kellner & Attorps, 2020; Kirschner et al., 1996; Sang et al., 2021; Waitoller & Artiles, 2013), where co-reflection plays crucial roles in constructing teachers' identities (El Nagdi et al., 2018; Yuan & Burns, 2017), deepening senses of ownership of change (Pyhältö et al., 2014) and building transformative capacity for school development and curriculum change (Liu, 2015).

Looking back, educators and teaching professionals have been vocal in demand for innovative programs and creative practices in education. Simultaneously, these advocates have acknowledged that teachers and schools must work together and harness their wisdom to implement new initiatives and innovations successfully to realize the promise of new practices for a dynamic, changing education world. Teacher collaboration in the form of university-school partnership (Ndunda et al., 2017) and cross-disciplinary partnerships (Hoachlander & Yanofsky, 2011) has been a key highlight in successful educational programs and practices (e.g., Kilpatrick & Fraser, 2019). Previous studies showed that teacher engagement in working as a team had positive impacts on fostering transformative pedagogy and innovative practice (Stoll et al., 2006), giving teachers ample opportunities to grow professionally and learn about, experiment, and assess student learning. Undoubtedly, the value of school-university partnership is in its enablement of building a learning community in which school practitioners, education professionals, and academics work together. The hope, then, is that teachers within and beyond their schools can inquire, innovate, and improvise educational practices in the current curricula through structured (contrived) collaboration and collaborative partnerships with experienced educators and experts from universities and relevant industries. In this connection, there have been strong requests for continuous team-based teacher inquiry to encourage sustainable in-depth teacher professional learning and innovative practices. It is time for us to rethink and understand how education can be strategically strengthened and structured through "teacher collectives" to create practical, evidence-based learning experiences and pursue effective, continuous improvement in (school-based) curriculum development.

## REFLECTION

Putting theory (thinking) into practice (doing) is a great emphasis in teacher education and professional development (Korthagen & Kessels, 1999). Learning by doing is unquestionably important; collaboration is a catalyst for making educational change and thus student learning and professional growth. However, "thinking" plays a far more important role in navigating and negotiating shared meanings and common understandings of collective action (research) and collaboration within and across the complex educational systems around the (global) community at large (Ravitch & Wirth, 2007).

Getting back to the connection between passion, action, and collaboration, I judge that the idea of "teacher collectives" is not just about the technical side but also the personal (human) side. There reflection plays a vital role in adequately engaging teachers in critical thinking and building deep knowledge when determining and deciding what to do and not to do. This reflection is a critical one, which is basically "the question of the justification for the very premises on which problems are posed or defined in the first place" (Mezirow, 1990, p. 12).

"Critical" reflection assists teachers in making professional judgments on actions and behaviors and building on ideas through three types of reflection: reflection-in-action, reflection-on-action, and reflection-for-action (Moghaddam et al., 2019; Schön, 1983). In so doing, teachers, locally and globally, engage in dialogues as a form of critical reflection for connecting thinking (theory) and action (practice). Dialogue makes collective teacher thinking happen by recapturing and reorganizing memories and reflecting on behaviors and actions in an open, constructive shared space to enrich and extend teachers' deep understandings and thus improve, stimulate, and sustain (good) practice in classrooms and schools. This has to be done under systematic and careful planning and facilitation of group inquiry, where space and time are taken into account in regulating teachers' thinking (Leung et al., 2020; Liu 2015; Orchard et al., 2016; Smyth, 1989; Winch et al., 2015).

Empowerment should be greatly appreciated and made explicit and readily accessible to teachers, teacher educators, and education researchers to support and articulate the efforts of curriculum development and school improvement, where teachers are encouraged and expected to take charge of deliberate decisions, try new ideas and challenges, and tease out the transformative potentials under the cultures of teacher leadership that respect and reinforce teacher autonomy and professionalism (Demir, 2015; Orchard & Wan, 2019).

In conclusion, the combination and interconnection of passion, action, collaboration, and reflection are expected to interdependently flourish and nourish the sustainable and strategic development of "teacher collectives" in managing innovation and facing the challenges of a dynamic and complex world.

## REFERENCES

Bernard, R. (2002). The passionate teacher: A practical guide. *Harvard Educational Review, 72*(4), 564.

Catelli, L. A., Costello, J., & Padovano, K. (2000). Action research in the context of a school–university partnership: Its value, problems, issues and benefits. *Educational Action Research, 8*(2), 225–242.

Chang-Tik, C., & Goh, J. N. (2020). Social and cognitive dimensions of collaboration in informal learning spaces: Malaysian social science students' perspectives. *Interactive Learning Environments*, 1–15.

Colucci-Gray, L., Das, S., Gray, D., Robson, D., & Spratt, J. (2013). Evidence-based practice and teacher action-research: A reflection on the nature and direction of "change." *British Educational Research Journal, 39*(1), 126–147.

Day, C. (2004). *A passion for teaching*. Routledge.

Demir, K. (2015). The effect of organizational trust on the culture of teacher leadership in primary schools. *Educational Sciences: Theory and Practice, 15*(3), 621–634.

Fransson, G., & Grannäs, J. (2013). Dilemmatic spaces in educational contexts–towards a conceptual framework for dilemmas in teachers work. *Teachers and Teaching, 19*(1), 4–17.

Hargreaves, A. (2005). Educational change takes ages: Life, career and generational factors in teachers' emotional responses to educational change. *Teaching and Teacher Education, 21*(8), 967–983.

Hayashi, A., & Tobin, J. (2015). *Teaching embodied*. University of Chicago Press.

Hazari, Z., Cass, C., & Beattie, C. (2015). Obscuring power structures in the physics classroom: Linking teacher positioning, student engagement, and physics identity development. *Journal of Research in Science Teaching, 52*(6), 735–762.

Hoachlander, G., & Yanofsky, D. (2011). Making STEM real. *Educational Leadership, 68*(6), 60–65.

Hobbs, L. (2012). Examining the aesthetic dimensions of teaching: Relationships between teacher knowledge, identity and passion. *Teaching and Teacher Education, 28*(5), 718–727.

James, M., & McCormick, R. (2009). Teachers learning how to learn. *Teaching and Teacher Education, 25*(7), 973–982.

Kellner, E., & Attorps, I. (2020). The school–university intersection as a professional learning arena: Evaluation of a two-year action research project. *Teacher Development, 24*(3), 366–383.

Kilpatrick, S., & Fraser, S. (2019). Using the STEM framework collegially for mentoring, peer learning and planning. *Professional Development in Education, 45*(4), 614–626.

Kirschner, B. W., Dickinson, R., & Blosser, C. (1996). From cooperation to collaboration: The changing culture of a school/university partnership. *Theory into Practice, 35*(3), 205–213.

Korthagen, F. A., & Kessels, J. P. (1999). Linking theory and practice: Changing the pedagogy of teacher education. *Educational Researcher, 28*(4), 4–17.

Leung, S., Wan, S. W. Y., Orchard, J., & Davids, N. (2020). Consolidating pre-service teachers' metacognition of online dialogue through visual methods: A Hong Kong case study. *Journal of Education for Teaching, 46*(5), 693–696.

Lieberman, A. (2000). Networks as learning communities: Shaping the future of teacher development. *Journal of Teacher Education, 51*(3), 221–227.

Liu, P. (2015). Motivating teachers' commitment to change through transformational school leadership in Chinese urban upper secondary schools. *Journal of Educational Administration, 53*(6), 735–754.

Mezirow, J. (1990). How critical reflection triggers transformative learning. In J. Mezirow and Associates (Eds.), *Fostering critical reflection in adulthood* (pp. 1–20). Jossey-Bass.

Moghaddam, A. K., Khankeh, H. R., Shariati, M., Norcini, J., & Jalili, M. (2019). Educational impact of assessment on medical students' learning at Tehran University of Medical Sciences: A qualitative study. *BMJ Open, 9*(7), e031014.

El Nagdi, M., Leammukda, F., & Roehrig, G. (2018). Developing identities of STEM teachers at emerging STEM schools. *International Journal of STEM Education, 5*(36), 1–13.

Ndunda, M., Van Sickle, M., Perry, L., & Capelloni, A. (2017). University–Urban high school partnership: Math and science professional learning communities. *School Science and Mathematics, 117*(3–4), 137–145.

Ng, P. T., Lim, K. M., Low, E. L., & Hui, C. (2018). Provision of early field experiences for teacher candidates in Singapore and how it can contribute to teacher resilience and retention. *Teacher Development, 22*(5), 632–650.

Orchard, J., Heilbronn, R., & Winstanley, C. (2016). Philosophy for Teachers (P4T)–developing new teachers' applied ethical decision-making. *Ethics and Education, 11*(1), 42–54.

Orchard, J., & Wan, S. W. Y. (2019). Philosophy, critical reflection and the development of teacher leadership in teacher education, East meets West. In M. Peters (Ed.), *Encyclopedia of teacher education*. Springer Nature.

Owen, S. (2014). Teacher professional learning communities: Going beyond contrived collegiality toward challenging debate and collegial learning and professional growth. *Australian Journal of Adult Learning, 54*(2), 54–77.

Owen, S. (2016). Professional learning communities: Building skills, reinvigorating the passion, and nurturing teacher wellbeing and "flourishing" within significantly innovative schooling contexts. *Educational Review, 68*(4), 403–419.

Owen, S. M. (2015). Teacher professional learning communities in innovative contexts: "Ah hah moments," "passion" and "making a difference" for student learning. *Professional Development in Education, 41*(1), 57–74.

Pyhältö, K., Pietarinen, J., & Soini, T. (2014). Comprehensive school teachers' professional agency in large-scale educational change. *Journal of Educational Change, 15*(3), 303–325.

Ravitch, S. M., & Wirth, K. (2007). Developing a pedagogy of opportunity for students and their teachers: Navigations and negotiations in insider action research. *Action Research, 5*(1), 75–91.

Robertson, D. A., Padesky, L. B., & Brock, C. H. (2020). Cultivating student agency through teachers' professional learning. *Theory into Practice, 59*(2), 192–201.

Sandholtz, J. H. (2002). Inservice training or professional development: Contrasting opportunities in a school/university partnership. *Teaching and Teacher Education, 18*(7), 815–830.

Sang, G., Zhou, J., & Muthanna, A. (2021). Enhancing teachers' and administrators learning experiences through school–university partnerships: A qualitative case study in China. *Journal of Professional Capital and Community, 6*(3), 221–236.

Schon, D. A. (1983). *The reflective practitioner: How professionals think in action*. Basic Books.

Sheridan, L. (2019). "A passion and enthusiasm to bring out the best in all": Regional candidate teacher motivations. *Australian Journal of Teacher Education, 44*(12), 81–101.

Smyth, J. (1989). Developing and sustaining critical reflection in teacher education. *Journal of Teacher Education, 40*(2), 2–9.

Somekh, B., & Zeichner, K. (2009). Action research for educational reform: Remodelling action research theories and practices in local contexts. *Educational Action Research, 17*(1), 5–21.

Søreide, G. E. (2006). Narrative construction of teacher identity: Positioning and negotiation. *Teachers and Teaching: Theory and Practice, 12*(5), 527–547.

Souto-Manning, M. (2012). Teacher as researcher: Teacher action research in teacher education. *Childhood Education, 88*(1), 54–56.

Stoll, L., Bolam, R., McMahon, A., Wallace, M., & Thomas, S. (2006). Professional learning communities: A review of the literature. *Journal of Educational Change, 7*(4), 221–258.

Tsang, K. K. (2019). Teachers as disempowered and demoralised moral agents: School board management and teachers in Hong Kong. *British Journal of Educational Studies, 67*(2), 251–267.

Tsui, A. B., & Law, D. Y. (2007). Learning as boundary-crossing in school–university partnership. *Teaching and Teacher Education, 23*(8), 1289–1301.

Waitoller, F. R., & Artiles, A. J. (2013). A decade of professional development research for inclusive education: A critical review and notes for a research program. *Review of Educational Research, 83*(3), 319–356.

Waitoller, F. R., & Kozleski, E. B. (2013). Working in boundary practices: Identity development and learning in partnerships for inclusive education. *Teaching and Teacher Education, 31*, 35–45.

Winch, C., Oancea, A., & Orchard, J. (2015). The contribution of educational research to teachers' professional learning: Philosophical understandings. *Oxford Review of Education, 41*(2), 202–216.

Yuan, R., & Burns, A. (2017). Teacher identity development through action research: A Chinese experience. *Teachers and Teaching, 23*(6), 729–749.

Zhu, G., Rice, M., Rivera, H., Mena, J., & Van Der Want, A. (2020). "I did not feel any passion for my teaching": A narrative inquiry of beginning teacher attrition in China. *Cambridge Journal of Education, 50*(6), 771–791.

# About the Authors

**Maria Impedovo**, PhD, is associate professor at ADEF Laboratory, Aix-Marseille University, France. Since 2014, she has taught at the School of Education (INSPE) at Aix-Marseille University, France. She received her PhD in educational technology in 2013. Her main research interests are identity, teacher agency, and teacher professional development. Since 2010, she has actively participated in multiple national and international formative and research projects. She has written scientific papers in Italian, Spanish, French, and English.

**Karen Ferreira-Meyers**, associate professor, is the coordinator of linguistics and modern languages at the Institute of Distance Education in the University of Eswatini (Southern Africa). She is also a research fellow of the University of the Free State (South Africa). She holds four master's degrees and a PhD in French and Francophone autofictional writing. She is a keen translator and interpreter. She publishes widely and regularly in various fields of research, among them the teaching and learning of languages; open, distance, and e-learning; online instruction and facilitation; autofiction and autobiography; crime and detective fiction; African literatures in European languages.

**Noriyuki Inoue**, PhD, is a professor at Faculty of Human Sciences, Waseda University, in Japan. He specializes in educational psychology and educational research methods. His recent research projects include teacher expertise development, social-emotional learning, educational innovation, lesson study, and action research methodology. He serves as a board member of the Japan Association of Research on Educator Transformation (JARET) and frequently serves as a consultant and adviser for schools and organizations across the world.

www.ingramcontent.com/pod-product-compliance
Lightning Source LLC
Chambersburg PA
CBHW032047300426
44117CB00009B/1224